'We can't rely on psychologists, philosophers, sociologists, or theologians to guide us at the very end. Only the painters, musicians, novelists and poets can give us calm entry into that mysterious night ...'

OLD OLD AGE
A BRIEF GUIDE

IAN HANSEN

ARCADIA

© Ian Victor Hansen 2018, 2020

First published 2018 by ARCADIA

the general books' imprint of

by Australian Scholarly Publishing Ltd

7 Lt Lothian St Nth, North Melbourne, VIC 3051

Tel: 03 9329 6963 / Fax: 03 9329 5452

enquiry@scholarly.info / www.scholarly.info

ISBN 978-1-925984-36-1

Cover design: Wayne Saunders

Grow old along with me!
The best is yet to be,
The last of life,
For which the first was made.
　　　　　Robert Browning

I grow old … I grow old …
I shall wear the bottoms of my trousers rolled.
　　　　　T.S. Eliot

Contents

Acknowledgements

Many thanks are due to Margaret and the late Peter Gill for all their on-going encouragement; to my grandson Tully and his wife Nina, for willing help in preparing the text for submission and IT advice generally; to Chris Wallace-Crabbe for his insightful and generous comments; to numerous friends who said I was on the right track; and to Bruce Dawe and UWA Publishing for permission to include his poem 'Walking Our Dog'. But most thanks go to my wife of over sixty years, Dorothy, for putting up with my bursts of obsessive writing and for being always able to put me right when I was wrong.

– 1 –

The Surprise of Ageing

For some reason he'd been having over the last few months a series of vivid dreams, all of them derived from actual memories. He was bushwalking across a steep range in the alps, he was on an overnight train in midwinter Germany with the snow in the lights from the carriages, he served three aces in a row in a tennis tournament, he was on his own laying a brick patio, on his fiftieth birthday he was jogging as usual around the local park, and now he was awake.

He threw back the doona and swung his legs over the side of the bed. He levered himself into a sitting position and wriggled his feet into his slippers. Then he went to stand, and after two fruitless lurching attempts, finally his knees supported him into being erect, though swaying a little. A sharp narrow pain across his lower back made him gasp softly and he began to shuffle to the kitchen, screwing his eyes tightly into focus. He put the kettle on, spooned instant coffee into two mugs, added milk, and shuffled with them back to the bedroom. The pain in his back was gone. 'It's a sunny morning, dear,' he said to his wife, still dozing. 'It could be a nice day.' His trembling hand, with concentrated care, placed her mug on the bedside table …

We are born, survive childhood and adolescence, rush into adulthood and never think that life will end, but past the biblical threescore years and ten we begin to wonder.

I regularly read newspaper reports that run something like this: 'an elderly pedestrian was struck by a car in Collins Street. The man, aged 67, was crossing …' What is elderly? 'The elderly couple in their 70s managed to escape the fire…' Geriatrics journals tend to distinguish three categories: the young old (65 years to 74), the old (75 to 84) and the old old (85+). When, however, my eye is caught by an article on old age I find the piece almost always deals with issues to do with people aged in their late 60s or their 70s, as though that makes them old. What happens next? We die? I'm in my late 80s. I can still feel very alive. Why don't more people write about octogenarians? What's it like to be an octogenarian? Studies on old age tend to be sociological in nature, dealing with cultural differences, often with an emphasis on medical issues and nursing homes and illustrated with graphs and statistics. This is not that kind of book.

I'm not myself one of those rudely healthy oldies who plays tennis twice a week. I have been visited by a number of ailments. It's true that I've never had knee or hip surgery, or skin or prostate cancer, but I've lived with the aftermath of polio from age 10, coeliac disease from 70, quadruple heart bypass from 80, with an auto-immune condition. Oh, and I've had cataract operations and I wear hearing aids. I was a secondary school English teacher and then a University academic.

What I'm trying to do in this brief guide is to set down how it is for one octogenarian. I think I have my wits about me. I'm wanting to explore how we can do old old age and what we have to deal with. Once the 60s and 70s are gone, what then? We are forced to choose between lamenting or celebrating our age. Our age has become an attitude, an adjustment, a transition of a kind that we've never had to deal with before. What I want to do here is to document something of the life of the old old. It is my hope that elderly readers will feel that I've got it right for them and also that the children and younger friends of those elderlies will have some appreciation of what it's like to be really old.

One of the significant conundrums of ageing is achieving a living balance between a failing body and a lively mind. It's well put by Vita Sackville-West in her 1930s novel, *All Passion Spent*. The Earl of Slane after a distinguished career in public life has just died at the age of 94. His six children now begin to wonder what they are going to do with their mother, the 88-year-old Lady Slane. Lady Slane had all her life been gracious, gentle, submissive and her children all expected she would spend the rest of her days staying with them in turn. But no, their mother makes it clear that she intends to live her own life according to her own inclinations. She wants no visits from her children or grandchildren and moves into a small house in Hampstead with her old French maid. The day she took up residence she wondered whether

perhaps she was one of those people on whom a contin-
uous acquaintance with strange countries makes little
impression – they remain themselves to the end; or perhaps she was really getting old. At the age of eighty-eight
one might be permitted to say it. This consciousness,
this sensation, of age was curious and interesting. The
mind was as alert as ever, perhaps more alert, sharpened
by the sense of imminent final interruption, spurred
by the necessity of making the most of remaining time;
only the body was a little shaky, not very certain of its
reliability, not quite certain even of its sense of direction,
afraid of stumbling over a step, of spilling a cup of tea;
nervous, tremulous; aware that it must not be jostled, or
hurried, for fear of betraying its frail inadequacy… Yet,
going up to Hampstead alone, she did not feel old; she
felt younger than she had felt for years, and the proof of
it was that she accepted eagerly this start of a new lap in
life, even though it be the last.

An aspect of old old age not often considered is the
clear possibility that despite bodily frailty, being afraid of
spilling a cup of tea, the mind is perhaps more alert than
it used to be. That's why Lady Slane doesn't feel old; that's
why numbers of my friends don't feel their age. The mind is
our safety. This is not to believe that the aged can be lumped
together in some homogeneity: the elderly have certain col-
lective features like age-related disabilities (deafness, failing
sight) but they are nevertheless as distinct from one another
as people of any age. Stereotyping does real harm in the real
world, especially with regard to the old.

So I'm setting down here how it is for one octogenarian

in the hope that it may be possible to extrapolate into other lives. 'Funny, it's not at all like that for me', or 'Oh yes, that's just the way it is'. More than anything else I want to be honest, which is the only way to truth.

First of all we need to remind ourselves of how we got here. Our generation has probably had to survive more change than any other in recorded history. There have been dramatic shifts in society's behaviours, both domestic and community; changes in political thinking and economic theory; constant movement in scientific research in areas such as medicine and molecular structures; and perhaps most mind-boggling of all, technological advancements. There are some of our generation who have been able to accommodate the cyber world and can make use of IT skills to simplify living, but there are also many of us who can't and find dealing with a high-tech society quite threatening. However, for all the changes we've had to deal with it's been the pace of those changes that's affected us most.

We need also to explore the ways our physical frailties lead on to emotional frailties, and what are the expectations we may have of ageing. There is the issue of growing old with a partner and other family members, and the importance of community and ways of holding on when our grip on life weakens. Finally, we have to face up to last things: what can we find to sustain us as the shadows really begin to lengthen?

Some years ago, dear friends of ours gave us a gift of

Daniel Klein's *Travels with Epicurus*; they thought we might find it interesting and even helpful. They had. Klein is an American author trained in philosophy and his little book has a rather lengthy subtitle, 'A Journey to a Greek Island in Search of an Authentic Old Age'. He questions the compulsion to want to remain ever young and wants to know if it is possible to be happy and fulfilled as an old man. He makes his way to the island of Hydra with a suitcase of philosophy books, including the works of Epicurus, looking for the secret of meaningful last days. After the title page is the following quotation from Epicurus:

> It is not the young man who should be considered
> fortunate but the old man who has lived well, because
> the young man in his prime wanders much by chance,
> vacillating in his beliefs, while the old man has docked
> in the harbor, having safeguarded his true happiness.

It's a delightful journey Klein takes us on. He's a witty and amusing writer, and through him we meet a wonderful array of elderly characters on the island. He presents us with a thoughtful meditation on the fully lived life.

But he tells us that at the time of writing he was 73; that is, in our terms, he was young old. This would explain how his view of this world begins to change as he draws to the final chapters of his odyssey. He introduces the idea of old old age. This was new to me, I have to admit. I'd never heard the junction of the two olds and I suddenly realised that it's what I am: old old. Fair enough so far. But

Klein hasn't been there yet, he's not lived the crucial decade into the eighties. He accepts the caricature of the old old as being 'second childishness and mere oblivion/Sans teeth, sans eyes, sans taste, sans everything' as Shakespeare put it. Klein imagined or imagines old old age means senility, and incontinence, and fits of anger and despair, and goes so far as to say that 'old old age stinks. It is horrible. The quality of life is usually zero'.

Wrong. He's wrong. There are many men and women in their eighties who suffer from chronic conditions that leave them fatigued and in pain, impatient with their bodies and restless at the prospect of little relief, counting the hours by the next round of medication; but there are also many elderly men and women who are able to greet each new day with at least some expectation that it may have pleasure in it. Old old age doesn't have to stink; it doesn't have to be horrible; it can be fulfilling or, as some would say, authentic. Of course there'll be disappointments and difficulties, sorrows and fears, but little that hasn't been part of life already.

Lots of middle-class professionals and people from commerce and business recognise the dangers of retiring – bang! – like that. One day they're in full time work, the next they've nothing to do. More often, new retirees organise casual work to ease themselves into full retirement. They pick up consultancies, or cover for people on long service leave, or set up little part-time projects. This is all very sensible. For nearly ten years after retirement my wife Dorothy and I as joint authors wrote on commission a number of institutional histories and biographies. Although labour-intensive, it was interesting work with comparatively little stress, and entailed travel that we otherwise would never have contemplated. I was much the same age as Daniel Klein when he wrote *Travels with Epicurus*. At the end of this period I was young-old plus, and paid employment was over. When you're living life, contributing to society and feeling positive about yourself, you don't have time usually to think about old age. For me, I was just happy being myself. I thought I had no more major decisions to make, no more pressing plans to enact. I could dress for comfort, wear jeans and open-necked shirts; up to a point looks didn't matter all that much any more. The garden became more important to me, a kind of gentle responsibility. What was opening out before me was a vista of soft and rolling hills. So this was old age.

As a couple, our contentment was such that we apparently must have given off an air of tranquillity. Our grown-up family found us self-sufficient. From young-old to old, though, I found I'd reached a point when I had to watch out for a range of behaviours and attitudes that had become more marked in my daily existence. I would be aware that something requires to be done, like a daisy in the garden needing to be staked up, and having thought about it I would then believe that I'd done it until a week later I noted it again and saw that I hadn't done it. I found myself therefore getting guilty about things not done that I promised myself I would do. I was becoming more and more forgetful and needing to make lists and then forgetting to consult the lists. I was feeling sorry for myself and getting borderline-possessive about health issues. I was trying to be cheerful all the time and I couldn't be. I hated feeling I was wasting a day, but I often didn't have the energy to do anything. So this was old age, on the edge of old old. If I can trust an old notebook of mine, I think it was Leon Trotsky who said, 'Old age is the most unexpected of all the things that can happen to a man.' My notebook tells me it was a diary entry. Wherever it's to be found, whoever said it, it's a helpful thing to say; old age is certainly a surprise.

It's true and it may come upon us suddenly that we don't think much about it until we're there. What we've had to inform us is a range of caricatures, of exaggerated images of the elderly, people uncertain on their feet, dozing in armchairs, sometimes benign, sometimes crabby, purveyed by comic strips, films, novels and TV sketches.

On the verge of old age, we like to imagine it (for ourselves, about to enter it) as having a romantic glow. Many of us remember – in Dickens's *Great Expectations* – John Wemmick's father, referred to lovingly as 'The Aged P', and the portrayal of the old man's benevolence and amiability. It's a comforting portrayal of ageing. We've all caught glimpses of an elderly couple in deep friendship sitting in a corner in intimate conversation and the laughing busload of nursing home residents on an outing.

But what is unexpected about old age is the way it

swings us between extremities. Communities are often blessed with variants of Aged Ps, but old old age especially also and often surprises us with unaccountable experiences of loneliness and disappointments, sorrows and emptiness, and an almost inevitably weakened physical state.

Florida Scott-Maxwell, American playwright, suffragette (!) and social analyst commented in 1968, when she was 85,

> Age puzzles me. I thought it was a great time. My
> 70s were interesting and fairly serene, but my 80s are
> passionate. I grow more intense as I age. To my own
> surprise, I burst out with hot conviction … I must calm
> down. I am far too frail to indulge in moral fervour.

Extremities, again. The old old are not always disappointed and lonely and weak. They can be vital and astonishingly strong.

As we age, it ought to be easier for us to be honest. We should be prepared to say it like it is. This is one of old age's great freedoms: we don't any longer have to tiptoe around ideas and opinions. So let's say that a happy retirement may be a cruel myth: we can only know happiness and contentment when we creatively contribute to the world, however restricted physically or socially that world may be, and we are not alone, those of us who are 85+, the old olds. In Australia there are near enough to 2,000,000 of us. We are a mixed bag: some of us have remained in our own homes, where we've been for thirty, forty years or more; some of us have downsized and moved into a unit or an apartment; some of us are free to live our lives as we wish; some of us have ongoing responsibilities for disabled children or siblings; some of us spend our days in the knowledge that we are surrounded by family and friends ready to give us assistance and company; some of us live alone with a cat or a dog.

Arguably it's probably the best time in history to be old. The practice of medicine has become so skilled that it increases life expectancy decade by decade; local government provides a range of supports which allow the elderly to remain in their own homes; in major cities and country towns there are retirement villages and nursing homes to cater for a whole range of individual needs. The elderly become less prone to anxiety, despair, depression and anger.

What happens as we age is that we shift towards appreciating everyday pleasures and relationships, like kind, welcoming words from a shopkeeper, and away from getting and achieving. We sometimes catch ourselves unaware and wonder why we've taken so long to appreciate these things. It's a lesson hard to grasp: that living is a learned skill and what can be the calm and wisdom of old age is only achieved over time. There are in fact lots of positives to be found in the lives of the old old. Being is more important than doing. The present is more important than the future. When we move into the eighties it's all change; through the years of the young olds and the olds, life throbs away much as it used to – a bit slower, perhaps, but still with some remnant vigour. Then it all begins to fall apart. It's why journalists, TV panellists and social commentators deal with issues of the young old and the old: they can't face the world of the old old. It's unnerving to them, because they see people in their eighties getting sick, forgetting things, having falls, withdrawing, and they'd rather not deal with it. Better to ignore it.

I remember that years ago (a long time ago?) someone came up with the bright idea of establishing what would be called a Council of Elders. This would be a national body made up of retired luminaries – Nobel Prize scientists, High Court judges, business tycoons, literary figures and the like. This Council of lively eighty-year olds would be a sounding-board for public opinion and would offer considered judgements about future aims and goals for Australian society. Names were canvassed and in fact announced. It's all a bit vague in my memory now and I can't recall the council ever meeting (I suppose it did); what sticks in my mind is that this group, once the fanfare had faded, never got established. It got ignored. The members were too old, what would they really have to offer? Who needs the opinions of the elderly? This is the age of youth and before year's end the council was quietly forgotten – too old.

The truth now is that the old old are doing better than most of us think. The threat of imminent sickness is not a terror; as people become aware of the finitude of their lives, as they recognise the horizon is shrinking, they don't ask for much, they aren't interested in building bigger barns to house their possessions, they're not after more power and control, they ask only to be able as far as possible to keep hold of the story of their lives, to make choices for themselves, and to relate to others on their own terms. They're happy being themselves.

So what, if a third of the eighty-plus cohort often feel sad or depressed – they're just tired, okay? The general public think or believe that illness, loneliness and dependence preclude the old old from any autonomy, any life of their own. Calling this period 'the golden years' is rank sentimentality, suitable only for the text of a greeting card; but on the other hand, there may be something more than a grain of truth in 'you're never too old to feel young'.

So how have the old olds come to be here?

– 2 –

How Did We Get Here?

One of my earliest memories is of my father crunching up our driveway with his face wreathed in smiles: he'd been up the street to a neighbour's and for the first time had heard with headphones a wireless description of a Test match. The neighbour's then primitive apparatus had given voice to the Bodyline test in Adelaide. The Australian Broadcasting Commission had been established only six months before. But today my grandchildren can *watch* a Test match on a mobile phone held in the palm of their hands.

Those of us who've survived into our eighth decade have had to adjust to an ever-increasing rate of change. Even domestic technology changed quickly. I remember our Coolgardie safe for keeping perishables fresh. This was a galvanised iron cupboard on legs, covered in hessian, the hem of which rested in a trough of water. By osmosis, the cupboard was surrounded by an evaporative shroud which had a cooling effect on the butter or milk or whatever was stored there. It was years before we had an ice chest, a wooden storage cupboard lined with zinc on top of which was a lidded compartment for a block of ice, delivered regularly by the ice man with his horse and cart. The next leap forward was a refrigerator powered by kerosene and later electricity. Now we have fridges with freezing cabinets that produce crushed ice at the press of a button.

Out in the laundry on Mondays my mother set a kindling fire under the copper, heating the water to boiling point. Heavy clothes like sheets and towels were lifted steaming into one of the pair of concrete troughs and then fed through a hand-turned wringer to the other trough to remove most of the water. The washing was strung across the back garden on lines, for this was a decade and more before the Hills Hoist. The comfort of seeing washing ballooning and waving on the line in a stiff breeze has been largely lost with the advent of our washing machines and dryers. These days some clothes never see fresh air or sunlight: it's off to the dry cleaners.

And so it went: recorded music from 78 rpm vinyl to 33 1/3s to audio tapes to CDs and who knows what next. There were clunky typewriters and then electric ones and then to word processors and computers and printers. But it hasn't been only technological change that we've had to adjust to. In my teens listening to a symphony on 78s meant getting up half a dozen times to turn the records over.

When I was growing up there was no locking of the house when you slipped down to the corner shop. I didn't know anyone at high school who didn't go either to church or Sunday School. Our pleasures were simple: I was in the Boy Scouts and had an arm-full of Proficiency Badges (Axemanship and Invalid Cookery were two I remember). Even well into our teens we spent much of our leisure time out of doors (there was no TV or Internet) and I genuinely don't remember being ever conscious of social divisions. Our food was simple (roast lamb, corned beef, potatoes, cabbage, no broccoli or bok choy). We were careful with money, a result of the Depression: there was rarely anything to spare and holidays were never lavish. One of my weekend chores was to chop the wood for the week (O, axeman!), wood for the laundry copper, the water heater in the bathroom, the stove in the kitchen, and in winter for the fireplace in the sitting room.

Our generation was just too young for World War II (and just too old for National Service later). Nevertheless the war was very real to us. We had blackout curtains at our windows and Air Raid Wardens to check on us. Dad and I dug an air raid shelter in the back garden and covered it with corrugated iron and soil. We had food and clothing ration books and could buy no more than our allowance; in the Scouts we collected silver paper and old pots and pans 'for the War Effort' – I could identify Allied, German and Japanese aircraft from posters on my bedroom wall. How simple the war seems when drones can now seek out and destroy petrol supplies in the Afghan mountains from hundreds of kilometres away. What I do remember vividly is the celebration of VP day when Adelaide's King William Street was locked and jammed with screaming, cheering people: my ears still tingle at the memory of it.

I grew up sexually innocent: I think most of us did. As teenagers my friends and I kissed and fondled our girlfriends but never (as the phrase was) went the whole way. My wife and I took to our marriage bed virgins, but none of our children did and our grandchildren won't either. I was talking to a former school-friend of my daughter's about relationships among today's young. She had wondered whether a couple she knew were in a relationship and *her* daughter said, 'Mum, that's just sex: they're not good friends or anything'. That's an astonishing change, it seems to me. The Pill has had an influence well beyond contraception and has impinged on social behaviour in countless ways. For us, travelling across suburbs in search of female companionship was not easy. When I was at primary school there was only one motor vehicle in our street and that was a commercial van. I first owned a car at age 26. Prior to that I rode a push bike. Everywhere. In all weathers. I had no gears for hills or strong winds. I rode my bike to meet girlfriends several suburbs away and we went out on buses. Then after midnight I would ride my bike home again.

On the back of my wardrobe door I had a picture of Jane Russell (who was she? You may ask) and in a drawer a collection of cigarette cards of Test cricketers and League footballers but that was the limit of my awareness of what's now called celebrity. The only films we saw were American and I was in love with Jane Russell. All we knew of the cricketers and footballers we read on the back pages of the newspaper in reports of matches and games. Of their private lives we knew nothing, nor did we care. Now my generation has lived into a world where celebrity is the fare of dailies and countless garish magazines. I find Botoxed women and half-shaven men pouting at me from the front covers of glossy supplements and I don't even know who they are. Posses of journalists and photographers camp outside the mansions owned or rented by these people, hoping to be able to satisfy the public's hunger for a glimpse into the lives of the rich and famous. My friends and I can't understand any of it, this obsession with the unattainable.

But there are other changes that I am asked to adjust to and I can't. These changes have to do with my life with words. Call me conservative or reactionary yet my impatience is, I suppose, directed at carelessness or laziness in language and my sense that these are moral issues. Let me explain. I am close to admitting defeat in the case of the distinction between 'disinterested' and 'uninterested'. 'Uninterested' has all but disappeared from the lexicon. Don Watson has been with vigour drawing attention to our mangling of language but no one seems to have been listening. What follows is drawn from my own collection of horrors from ABC broadcasts. Misuse of words is one thing: 'he was appraised of this fact' ('apprised' surely?) and 'myriad of options' ('myriad' is adjectival, not a noun) but the thing that causes me to wince more than anything else is the lazy shifting of accent from one syllable to another: the American pronunciation of 'ceremony' is the most cringemaking, closely followed by 'research': in the former the accent should fall on the first syllable, in the latter, on the second. There are other lazy pronunciations with misplaced accents, words like 'clandestine', 'lamentable', 'comparable', 'corollary'. And there's further laziness in swallowing fricative t's into plosive d's, as in 'Labor Pardy' and 'udder devastation'.

Glib phrases abound in our language, so glib as to become meaningless like 'best practice', 'benchmarking', 'key performance indicators', 'impact factors'. And here are some of my treasures from speakers on ABC news bulletins: 'If the downturn gathers some legs, we may lose some wind in our sails'; 'it's all hi-guys and high-fives and that's real Australia' (like 'other companies are stepping up to the plate'?); 'we are remaining vigilant as to the unfolding circumstances'. A while ago I rang an emergency number to enquire about a power failure and was told by a recorded message that the energy company was 'experiencing intermittent technology issues'. What is someone of my generation to make of all this casual-speaking world?

Growing up, we were forming our lives in an unhurried and unharried way. We were free from stress. We were not competitive in the sense of wanting more things or better things than our friends. Sure, the latter years of the Depression marked us, made us perhaps socially unadventurous: we left school or university in the full expectation that we would get a job for life. We were a fortunate generation.

I believe we were a welcoming generation. I recall the influx into our society of the homeless and often stateless persons from a broken eastern Europe: Balts, we called them, for convenience. For a time I became involved with members of the Hungarian community in Adelaide; I coached three of its young men in an English language component in university entrance requirements. The family of two of them welcomed me into their circle with extraordinary warmth. The other one of them, a lost and lonely soul, came to my home often. All of them in due course became prominent members of Adelaide's professions. No nation on earth took in outsiders with so little fuss as we did. That's why my generation is at a loss to understand how our recent governments have shown so little compassion for asylum seekers, especially boat people. Vietnamese came by boat and were welcomed. What has changed us? Why am I ashamed in this matter to be Australian? I set this much down not to evoke sympathy for all that we didn't experience but merely to point out that adjusting to the changes that have come into our lives has not been easy. Coping with the last twenty years has been bad enough but we've had 70-odd years of change in our lifetimes. If we sometimes don't understand today's world it's not because we are grumpy old men and women. It's just because we are a little tired. It's all been a bit much and if we sometimes hanker after a simpler society it's an understandable yearning rather like Wordsworth's:

… Those first affections
those shadowy recollections …
Are yet the fountain light of all our day.

Speculating like this on how things used to be for me and my age-peers, I find I've disturbed a whole range of reminiscences making up my past. These 'shadowy recollections' are unbidden memories that mean at least something to me and are all part of where I've been. They come in a jumble. I am with my school friends milling on the pavement outside the local cinema waiting for the doors to open for the Saturday arvo screening which always included the next episode of the current thriller or Western. My children are asking me if they can have a Blue Heaven milkshake. With my stepmother in the school holidays I'm listening to the ABC radio serial 'Blue Hills'. I'm feeling quite sophisticated in my 20s as I choose between Ben Ean or Barossa Pearl for a dinner party for friends. None of these recollections would mean anything to my grandchildren: everything has changed.

Like the status of bank managers. In my day (to borrow a phrase) a bank manager enjoyed considerable social status and would be sought after for advice on a number of issues and not necessarily financial ones. They were trusted. In these days the situation is very different. There's a general loss of respect for more public figures. I may not have subscribed to their political philosophies, but I saw Bob Menzies as the Prime Minister and Tom Playford as the premier of South Australia and respected their titles; they also had about them moral certainty; you knew where they were coming from. I'm not sure that I now know where my political leaders come from. It's all a social shift I'm trying to adjust to.

And is it only me who finds common speech is being speeded up? It began with radio and TV spruikers advertising goods and services, spread to stand-up comics, then actors began speaking their lines more quickly and now it seems that all public utterances are hurried and rushed and even breathless. There's enough acceleration in social intercourse as it is without gabbling sentences together.

Some little while ago our two sons were visiting us. I can't remember the context of our conversation but one of them asked for the birth date of the Duke of Wellington. I said I could check it quickly ('I'm guessing the 1760s') and made to rise from my chair. 'Don't bother, Dad' said the other son, 'I'll ask Siri'. He produced his smart phone and said to it, 'Hey Siri, in what year was the Duke of Wellington born?' A brief pause and to my amazement this Siri said quite clearly '1769'. That's the kind of technology that my generation finds astonishing and even threatening. Are my grandchildren really carrying the sum of human knowledge in a slim electronic device that fits in their pocket?

I'm well aware that probably vast numbers of octogenarians are computer-literate. But not me. I don't even understand computer-language: what's a gigabyte, for heaven's sake? I'm embarrassed to talk with age-peers who can email photographs or newspaper articles. I can't do that.

Using our computer as a word-processor, I don't know how to shift a paragraph to a different page; I cut it up with scissors, paste it where I want it and photocopy it with my printer. I *have* found an octogenarian friend who can't send text messages from his phone. I can do that. I can text a grandchild with a flourish like 'How r u 2day?' ironically using a language not my own.

My IT incompetence does not, however, mean that I am unaware of the ramifications of all this high technology. We are all familiar with film clips of a production-line in a motor vehicle 'manufactory'. The very word 'manufactory' is a misnomer: in fact nothing is made 'by hand'. Computer programs have been devised to control screwdrivers and spanners to bolt panels to a chassis with no human intervention at all. Computers have brought automation to a fine pitch. In almost any manufacturing process computer-generated automation has replaced human workers. Before my children have reached my age there will be huge job losses due to automation and the creation of a 'useless class' comprising millions of former workers now devoid of any social value. But that's not all. Even from my standpoint of the IT innocent, I can see artificial intelligence threatening the middle-class because they have the jobs easiest to replace. I suffer the discomfort of living in a world strange to me. I find it difficult and painful to live in this world. It's because I have so much time to think about it. Certainly I reckon there'll never be an old old age like this one.

Sometime a little while back I came across a helpful book by Canadian journalist Michael Harris: it was called *The End of Absence*. What is immediately attractive about it is its (another one) rather lengthy subtitle: 'Reclaiming What We've Lost in the World of Constant Connection'. Harris points out that in these internet days we're in unrelenting touch with others, how there's no longer space in our lives for day-dreaming. We are more at ease with technologies than with each other. As Harris puts it bluntly, 'The phone is easy, people are hard'. We've become slaves to texting because voice-to-voice conversations have too many pitfalls. Human relating is proving to be too difficult and demanding. We apparently want to communicate at some remove. But we nevertheless want 'constant connection': that's why the first thing we do on waking up is to check our smartphone or our emails. And Harris can therefore observe that we don't see teenagers staring into space any more.

I pass a group of teenage schoolchildren waiting for a tram or a bus; they're not chattering together as we would have done in our day but are absorbed in their phones, thumbs busy, oblivious to those around them. I have been asking myself, how did I myself, how did we octogenarians get here? So this is where we've got to?

– 3 –

Losses

It's a truism that in Western societies individual human beings are living longer. People are getting older. I'm getting
old and it worries me that the elderly stride, shuffle or limp
into what is loosely called old age, and never really deal
with it. They hear voices telling them that old age is OK:
journalists point out there are more roles being written for
older TV and cinema actors, sociologists publish studies
of the sexual behaviour of the older generation, politicians
preach acceptance of senior members in the workforce. It's
all positive and upbeat.

But here's the rub: how old is old? An AFL footballer
in his early 30s is 'too old' to have his contract renewed; a
well-regarded novelist is almost 90 and is still producing
fine work. And there's another thing: at the beginning of
life a few years makes a huge difference – a girl of seven is
very different in a number of ways from a girl of ten. Towards the end of life a mere three years makes a similarly big

difference – a man of seventy-seven is very different from a man of eighty.

I find myself wondering for whom I'm setting down these reflections. I have myself done the sixties, retirement and all those adjustments. I've done the seventies, the physical frailties and the slowing down. What I think I wanted to do is to be honest about ageing. There's a lot of pretence about.

I suggested in the first chapter that accounts of issues of old age seem confined to the decades of the sixties and the seventies. When I talk to my age-peers I find that they think this is really the case. They, too, curious as they are about their circumstances, find themselves alerted by a newspaper article on old age and are disappointed that it is obviously written for a readership of baby boomers. Even when a journalist conducts his or her own little survey of attitudes of the elderly, the respondents are never older than the early seventies. What's with the octogenarians?

I have found one reference (one) in a newspaper magazine to an interview with an old old ager, David Malouf, one of Australia's most admired novelists and poets. 'I think you have to go slowly', he is quoted as saying:

> I'm well over 80. The older you get you realise there is
> a lot more time than you think. It's good to be patient.
> Allow yourself to attend very, very closely to what is
> going on. I think attention is actually the thing we need
> to bring to our own life and to other people.

That's the kind of positivity that you can find in the old olds. There is more time than we think and certainly we need to be attentive to the world we find ourselves in.

Old old age is a bit of a mixed bag, just like life as a whole, really. When we were younger and in the workforce we were affirmed in what we did and that made us feel we were contributing. Elderlies don't get much affirmation and we miss it. However, at the same time, we find our age has made us more open to reconciliation and we deal with things better.

In the first five years or so of my retirement I would run into friends who would greet me with 'How are things going with you, Ian? Busy?' To which I found myself answering, 'Trying not to be.' What is it with the early elderly that they feel guilty if they are not rushing about? It's probably even dangerous to stop dead (an interesting phrase) and daily do nothing after an active life but it's not impossible to find a point of balance. Going part-time is one option, finding casual work another. There's consultancy, though I've never been able to find out what that actually means. I was fortunate. The writing commissions Dorothy and I had gave us something to get up for in the morning, yet if we wanted to visit one of our children living interstate we could put our writing to one side. This arrangement eased us into full retirement. We never felt the need for the University of the Third Age or Probus Club. I know such programs serve a valuable purpose for many people but I wonder whether for the comfortable middle classes they don't result in or encourage a kind of competitiveness. It's all very well and understandable to travel to Moscow or Salzburg, but who's been to the Roman settlements on the North African coast? It's the busyness question again.

Remember how as young-olds and olds we were delighted to attend Grandparents' Days and sit on tiny chairs at the back of the room, or babysit while our children went out to dinner or even house-sat ('Who'll look after the cats?'), while the whole young family flew off to a holiday? All part of being busy.

The great unsaid in this little book is that despite the social and technological changes our world has experienced, one thing remains constant and that is human impulses. The restlessness of our age isn't new, much as we might want to believe it. Arnold Toynbee in an autobiography quoted the following passage; it is from Lucretius, poet-philosopher, who lived 99–55 BC:

> People seem to feel that there is a load on their minds
> that is wearying them with its weight. If only they could
> be as clearly aware of the causes of this and of the source
> of this massive malady in their hearts. If they could,
> they would not lead the kind of life that is so common a
> spectacle today. We see someone at a loss to know what
> he wants, and therefore perpetually seeking to be on the
> move, as if that would enable him to cast off his burden.
> Bored at home, he keeps on sallying out from his grand
> mansion, and then suddenly returns, having found that
> he feels no better out of doors. Driving his cobs, he
> rushes precipitately to his villa out in the country, with

the urgency of a fireman going to the rescue of a house on fire. He has no sooner reached the villa's threshold than he yawns; or he goes off into a heavy sleep and seeks relief in oblivion; or perhaps he heads hurriedly for the town and revisits that. In this way everyone is on the run from himself – a companion from whom he cannot escape in reality.

It's arresting to know this was written over two thousand years ago. It sounds so contemporary; people in their McMansions scuttling away to their holiday houses because they can't stay still; on the run from themselves. The young-old, the old and even the old old are inclined to seek safety from boredom in ongoing activity.

Ageing is often seen as something to be fearful of. It represents slowing down and that is to be avoided at all costs. If we can afford it, we travel. We keep on the move. Annually. Where are you going this year? The 70-year-olds especially get quite good at it. But do they ever reflect on why they do it? Of course travel can be engaging, instructive and refreshing, can become almost a hobby, but often it's a hastily assembled barrier against getting old. While we still have the physical capacity to travel, we can believe we're not ageing. Guided tours, especially in Europe and the Far East, take the stress out of hotel bookings and travel arrangements for trains and buses and you have the security of a party of like-minded companions. If you're more independent you put savings into a you-beaut caravan with every technological aid and join the grey nomad circuit around Australia for months at a time. You can store your photographic memories on your digital camera or your phone and flick them at yourselves or your friends on your return. What purpose does this activity serve? Are we to accept it as a concomitant of ageing irrespective? If we've been active all our adult lives, making money or serving segments of society, then we often don't want to recognise that busyness in old age is no longer a major impulse to living. There needs to be a shift in the way in which we order our days. But certainly that shift runs the risk, if we're not careful, of an enervating boredom. For example, my wife and I were long-time subscribers to a concert series. The subscription meant that we made friends with subscribers who sat either side and in front of us: it meant that we carried the concert home with us and found that it led us into other musical experiences. But eventually the knees that a full life had left us with found the walk from the car park and the steep steps in the concert hall to our seats had made concert-going a physical trial. With some sorrow we let our subscription lapse. As I think back, I wonder whether this decision wasn't the first forced upon us by ageing. After decades of concert-going, now suddenly the whole segment of what we must call however pompously our cultural practice had been sliced from our experience of our world. It was one of the first indications that we were facing a series of losses.

It used to be fashionable to invoke the Kubler-Ross stages of grieving to ease the confusion people felt when a loved one had died: the recognition of the emotional stages one passed through after experiencing loss was supposed to induce calm in those suffering grief. The five stages were 1. Denial, 2. Anger, 3. Bargaining, 4. Depression and 5. Acceptance and they made a lot of sense to a lot of people. Psychologists, sociologists and counsellors borrowed them to use for their own purposes. The stages were never intended to be linear and ordered but to represent the range of feelings that accompanies loss. Although initially the stages were to be applied to the trauma of dealing with the death of family or friends, they soon were used in relation to almost any circumstance of loss. For example, a married couple lose their family home through the legal enactment of compulsory purchase and have no option but to accept life in an apartment. But before they reach the stage of acceptance they are angry in their loss, angry because the triggers of memory have been taken from them, the bedroom where their two sons slept into their teens, the kitchen where major decisions were taken.

I was cross at losing those concert performances. I'd wanted our attendance at them to go on for, I don't know, forever or at least as far into the future as I could see. I got angry because I was going to have to learn to live without evenings that had become important to me. Maybe that's why the elderly often become cranky and grumpy. It's not only that the extraordinarily rapid changes in society and technology have left them weary of such a shifting world, but it's also that the losses in their lives over the years have left a residue of anger in the way they respond to what's going on around them. It's the reason why I flinch when I hear TV newsreaders mispronouncing words.

Whether it's the same for other generations or not I can't tell, but I used to believe that with old age came calmness and warmth. I suppose it had to do with the manner of the old people I used to visit. They sat back in a comfortable chair, they spoke softly and deliberately, they smiled rather than laughed. What they gave off was a sense of patience and even resignation, a mellowness. I remember two in particular, a widely read and highly intelligent former minister of religion and a tiny, sweet-faced archetypal great-grandmother. I used to wonder how it was these two had survived, given the length of their days. I put it down to the mellowness that came with age.

I've always been a fan of Julian Barnes, the British novelist and essayist. There's a wonderful elegance about his writing style and he's a shrewd observer of people in their relationships. In his 2011 novel, *The Sense of an Ending*, the principal character is a retiree trying to come to terms with his past. He reflects upon a woman he'd known for forty years and finds her unchanged across that period, and thinks:

> … why should we expect age to mellow us? If it isn't life's business to reward merit, why should it be life's business to give us warm comfortable feelings towards its end? What possible evolutionary purpose could nostalgia serve?

I don't find this cynical. Most of us growing older have had experiences that have taught us that we scarcely receive due reward for our contribution to either commerce or human relationships. We all, for instance, come to know broken friendships and such disappointments are lifelong. To dwell on the pleasurable past (as Julian Barnes seems to be suggesting) is no way to prepare oneself for inevitable discouragement.

Social myths have a high survival rate. Ideas like childhood is a happy time and stepmothers are unpleasant figures have been rooted in our perceptions of human life for centuries. Matching the received image of the nasty old witch, mean and toothless, is the contrary image of the benign and welcoming old lady with her knitting. Of course our preference is for the latter to be the kind of person we want to be as we age but that's not necessarily the way things evolve.

I find I have to fight against crankiness. I'd like to think people see me as a stereotypical mellow old man but I have to face the certain fact that a great deal of living has left me weary and impatient. It's said that as we age we should beware of reading only things we agree with. The point is clear. If we read only newspapers whose editorial position coincides with our own, for example, we'll never become aware of contrasting opinion. If we read only about issues we agree with, we'll never allow ourselves the luxury of changing our mind. It won't do simply to get cranky about things that go counter to our own views.

The most serious problem with ageing is closing of the

mind. It leads to smugness and self-satisfaction. It blunts judgement. Too many older people become locked into opinions and perceptions they have developed in their 60s and 70s and claim they lack the energy to see things any differently. That is an excuse. There is a simple way out. *Try* other things, at least. A new TV series is being promoted … it looks like it's not my cup of tea… but I'll try it out. The first episode is just what I thought it'd be, so I won't be watching that again. No great loss. Or the first episode was intriguing, so maybe I'll try again next week. Try a new title at the local library. Try that new restaurant. Get out of the rut of doing the shopping on Thursdays. Keep the mind open.

Michel De Montaigne, the French humanist, tried hard at it. He found it initially difficult to accept the inevitability of old age and complained that

> I should be grudging and ashamed if the wretchedness
> and misfortune of my decrepitude were rightly to set
> itself above my good, healthy, eager, vigourous years,
> and if men were to judge me not by where I have been
> but where I am no longer.

To have our reputation rest upon where we are no longer is a serious matter; it suggests that we have never advanced from where we were earlier in our lives. We need to have moved on. Old age mustn't mean we just stop and remain enslaved by ideals and ideas we previously found comfortable.

We are inclined to accept stereotypes of old age without criticism. Becoming young-old, baby boomers especially want to postpone ageing, because the images they have of the elderly don't suit them at all. Even those who are actually old are uneasy: they are beginning to realise that physical frailties lie not so far ahead.

– 4 –

Frailty

I have a neighbour nearing his 70s who's involved in the Masters Games movement. It's an annual series of athletic competitions for 'the elderly', for various age groups that range up into the 80s. It is open to both men and women. My friend's sporting interest is in swimming and over the years he's been awarded several gold and silver medals for his efforts. There are, apparently, sprint and middle-distance track events for runners, as well as discus and javelin competitions and jumps, in programs just like in meetings for youthful athletes in their prime. It reminds me of the so-called 'Golden Oldies', an international festival of 'elderly' Rugby Union players: there are, for example, modified rules for the matches and your age determines how long you may play in any one game. Tucked away in a corner of the sports pages of newspapers you may often find accounts of the exploits of elderly and sometimes very old golf and tennis players and marathon runners.

I have a sneaking admiration for these people. Age is not wearying them. Their discipline and determination is remarkable. But it's obviously their *thing*. It's not for everybody. It's their thing because of some genetic fluke, body-mass, sense of balance, lung capacity, heart-rate inherited from their forebears and honed regularly over decades. They have simply lasted a long time and have not been compromised by serious illnesses. A physiotherapist of some reputation once told me that she winces when she sees 80-year-olds working out in a gymnasium. At the onset of old age, vigorous exercise can only at best maintain muscle-tone and strength: it can't improve performance and by the age of 80 has no positive effect – it's all in their minds.

To live longer, to be actively healthy for longer is not a moral virtue. I've heard people say of an 80-year-old club tennis player, 'Isn't she amazing?' Well, no, she's not amazing. She's just fortunate. We may wish we were like her but we're not and never would've been.

When I was young, say in my late teens and early 20s, I only knew one 80-year-old. I knew people in their 70s and they, I thought, were about as old as you could get. Their grandparents died young in their 50s and 60s and they had survived because medical science had kept them going. My paternal grandfather reached 80 but that was thought to be 'a very good age': my maternal grandparents didn't make it out of 60. As a consequence, as I was growing up into adulthood, I didn't have much contact with the elderly. I couldn't conceive of what life was like for them and I felt awkward in their presence. I couldn't have known what growing old would mean to me. I never thought about it, of course, but I was facing the unknown. It's different for my grandchildren. They're all in their 20s and they've seen me and my wife age. They remember at the beach diving into waves with Gran'pa and playing ball games with Gran'ma in the back garden and now Gran'pa has to ask them to move a heavy pot plant to a new spot. They've been able to observe Gran'pa and Gran'ma in decline. They'll have an inkling at least of what old age means in a way I never knew.

I'm not here thinking of those elderly who ride their bicycles for scores of kilometres on country roads or hold their own in a singles tennis set, nor am I thinking of those who struggle with debilitating conditions like Parkinson's and Alzheimer's. It's the people like me, like most of my acquaintances, who wouldn't attract sympathy as they walked to the newsagent's, who look all right, who manage a barbecue or a drinks party. What can we expect as we age?

There are a lot of physical twinges that accompany ageing. Even getting out of bed in the mornings isn't as easy or simple as it once was. Your back has somehow stiffened and turning over requires an effort; getting the bedclothes folded back, the legs flung over the edge of the mattress and elbowing yourself to sitting erect, it's a real swing to straitening your spine; all this business is required before you begin to prepare for shifting your body weight from buttocks to knees and ankles and feet. There was once a time when all of this sequence of activities was achieved without conscious effort or planning. Now it takes longer. So does getting out of a chair, because you need a push-off with the heels of both hands. A low sofa, although comfortable to sit in, is difficult to get out of and will cost the embarrassment of two or three attempts to get to a standing position.

It's a trial getting in and out of seating because our physical frame fails us. What we could once do with ease we find arduous. In and out of a sofa was a simple act, but is now socially stressful, especially if we have to make a joke about our problem. Lots of tasks become a challenge, but we shouldn't forget that while the elderly may be frail, they are tenacious. They become imbued with a stubbornness that often leads to successful outcomes. In the 1981 movie, *On Golden Pond*, starring Katharine Hepburn and Henry Fonda, a contrast is drawn between a younger generation and an older couple. At one point, Fonda, playing the part of an acerbic retired professor, rages against his difficulties with the physical environment and snarls, 'Do you think it's funny being old? My whole goddam body's falling apart'. This angry sentiment goes on ringing through the heads of the elderly if they let it.

When I first started thinking about this book, I would spend three-quarters of an hour in the garden. I'm doing nothing strenuous. I rake the casuarina needles off the grass, I trim several lavender bushes after their flowering, I dead-head a large iceberg rose and then find I think I've had enough. I water some hanging baskets and that's it. My lower back is stiff, my knees ache when I bend over. It's not funny, being old. But I sit with a cup of coffee with my wife for fifteen minutes and I feel good about myself. I stroll around the garden and am pleased with what I've done. I think I'll have another potter in a day or two. Six months later I found I couldn't manage it any more.

One of the inevitabilities we must face as we age is that we have done more and more things for the last time. I've mown the lawn for the last time. I'll never mow it again. I've dug over the bed along the side fence for the last time. I've cleaned the roof gutters for the last time. What then catches us unawares is the finality that's implied. We've come to the end of a range of physical activities. We have to call on a daughter or a grandson to replace a light globe in the ceiling. That's hard for us, at first. For decades we lived as if we would go on forever. We never considered that our vitality and physical competence would ever desert us. But there were signs: I found that replacing a tap washer took me twice as long as it used to; my wife discovered that cleaning the kitchen floor took her longer than it used to and cost her more effort.

One of the things that's come with age and has crept up on me like a surprise is an awareness that my sense of balance is nothing like it was. Walking on an uneven surface is a bit tricky. In my back garden is a brick pathway which I myself laid thirty-five years ago and in the intervening period the roots of the nearby tree have caused the path to buckle unevenly. I have now to negotiate it with great care. I have to watch where I put my feet. It's not that my ankles feel that they might twist awkwardly. It's that the whole of my ability to keep myself steady is unsure. I even feel this balance thing when I'm walking around the house. I may sway a little but find myself putting a hand out to momentarily touch the certainty of a wall. I suppose it's why we so often hear it said that so-and-so has 'had a fall' or 'taken a fall'. I me myself personally have had some falls I must confess. They're a bit of an embarrassment, really, if all you get from them is a grazed elbow or a bruised knee. But falls are a worry: they may result in a serious injury. If I'm taking a significant walk, say around a suburban block, I now take a stick; it gives me some confidence and reminds me to take care and not walk heedlessly.

The late British novelist, Elizabeth Taylor, deserves to be better known than she is. Her *Mrs Palfrey at the Claremont* tells of an elderly widow who lived out her last years as a resident in a private hotel. She had just 'taken a fall' while out walking:

> Mrs Palfrey was trying to walk off a stiffness in her hip, but it would not be walked off. It seemed, instead, to be settling in, locking her joint, so that every step was consciously achieved. She realised that she never walked now without knowing what she was doing and concentrating upon it; once, walking had been like breathing, something unheeded. The disaster of being old was in not feeling safe to venture anywhere, of seeing freedom put out of reach.

'Disaster' is not too strong a word for most of us. Walking is like all those other things we've been doing automatically without thinking, reaching behind to close a gate, bending over to pick up a coin, stretching up to reach something on a shelf. It's become an effort of will; that is, we have to calculate our movements. The freedom that we once knew is out of reach.

With the loss of that freedom comes what is in some elderlies a fixation on frailty. They become overly interested in the superficial. They want to talk about their son's sprained wrist or their granddaughter's first tooth and very soon they're into health issues. Dorothy and I once invited to afternoon tea a couple we'd not seen for years. As they settled into easy chairs, the husband brightly said, 'Now, first of all, how's your health?' As though that was the most important thing to share.

With these physical frailties comes a kind of mental decline. Just as muscle tone in our limbs loses flexibility and we become slower and more uncertain in our movements, so, as we age, our thinking, our planning, our remembering slow. While it's probably true that the medication we take regularly may contribute to our mental slowing down, much of our dilatory behaviour has to be put down to ageing, simple as that. It's rare to find elderlies who never miss a beat. I find myself standing in the middle of the kitchen and in all seriousness asking myself, 'What did I come in here for?' Memory-fades like this become more and more common as people age. I'm fortunate. I have a partner in the house and I can call out, 'What did I come in here to do, dear?' It's so annoying, this kind of forgetfulness. It manifests itself in different ways. There's a tall weed in the garden bed near the front gate and for four days in a row I forget to pull it out. 'Did you ring Brian about that book you borrowed?' my wife asks, because I told her I'd do it tomorrow and it had 'escaped my mind', as they say. These peccadilloes of the ageing mental processes can be amusing or annoying depending on the circumstance but they are inescapably real. Is it because we become tired or lethargic or overly cautious?

Related to the forgetting of little things is telling the same story over and over again. Very often I want to interrupt a friend in full flight and say, 'Yes, you told me about that', or 'I've heard this before' but I don't have the courage, somehow. It seems hard on the storyteller because the tale is obviously important to him. I have on several occasions caught myself doing the same thing, repeating myself, telling the story a second time to the same audience; it's something I have to attend to.

We don't cope very well with the frailty that accompanies ageing. We are surrounded by commercial pressures to seek fitness and wellness. We don't like admitting to an increasing vulnerability in ourselves. Studies suggest that something like 44% of the 85+ cohort have to admit to being frail. That is, our reserves of confidence and strength decrease and leave us forever impaired. Age is not for the faint-hearted.

But who am I to be setting down these responses to my condition? What has life done to me as I've worked my way into the eighties? How have my opinions and attitudes been coloured by what's happened to me and my body? As with age my horizons have inevitably contracted and the future for me has become finite, my focus has shifted to the here and now in a way I'd not known before. I become, then, more and more aware of little things like the bending over and the reaching up. There are positives: almost half of the elderly population feel that life has turned out better than they thought it would. But I'm not so sure that those same elderlies ever imagined the daily nuisance of sudden tiredness or forgetfulness or mysterious aches. When I was young-old, I liked to look forward to being old or even old-old. I thought these later stages (if I got to live that long) would give me time to learn new things, to enlarge my circle of friends, to explore further my hobbies and pastimes. I never thought that my body would let me down to such an extent.

Frailty or mere awareness of frailty leads us to worrying and as we worry, we begin to fear our age: is this the end? Will we be able to face the daily activities even like getting dressed in the morning, getting those buttons done up or reaching behind to hook a bra strap into place: our fingers are not as clever as they once were. Coping with such silly frustrations makes some of us grumpy and impatient. Sometimes we sit on the edge of the bed and in our minds run back into the past when we could leap, yes, leap out of bed and scamper to the kitchen and put on the kettle. Because we can't do this any more, we wonder if we are becoming what bureaucrats call 'non-productive economic burdens'. We begin to have regrets about having come as far as we have. Are we of any real use? Having become frail?

There needs to be a way out of this. We've got to believe that as we age we can transcend all thoughts of limited views of life that we had when we were younger. We can let go of conflict: 'What's it matter?' and 'Let's not worry about it' can be helpful and legitimate responses. We may even take softer views of right and wrong. Things are not either black or white: in our everyday domestic moral world there are shades of grey.

I'm reminded of an exceedingly wise observation of the Dalai Lama's: 'Don't ask people what they believe; ask them how they cope'. How we cope is who we are.

– 5 –

Living with Frustrations

I'm not sure what expectations I had of ageing. The thing is that ageing doesn't occur with catastrophic suddenness: one day you're middle-aged and the next you're old. If you enjoy reasonable health you are not aware of growing old, although hurrying to catch a bus isn't perhaps as easy as it used to be. I remember in my 70s finding the uphill climb to the ninth green (why is the ninth always uphill?) more of an effort than it used to be. However, once my putter was in my hand and I was eyeing the hole, I forgot about the climb. Until the next time. That's how I aged, by almost imperceptible degrees. So I was fortunate.

Nevertheless, into my 80s those imperceptible degrees began to accumulate. My body had begun to stall. It took me longer to do things. I began to get used to what I'd have to call a kind of general lessening of capacity. But what worried me was that unless I was very careful I would soon slip into one of several characterisations of old age, become a cipher. For example, there's the musical hall version of the elderly, either the cranky computer-illiterate misery or the benign, quietly-spoken gracious guest or the quirky vivacious gleeful and ageless companion. It's a novelist who can reveal a really wearisome aspect of ageing. In Anita Brookner's *Private View*, the principal character, George Bland (an appropriate surname) reflects on his days:

> He recognised the signs of age, both in his largely pointless activity and his totally unearned inactivity. All he could hope to do was to keep them to himself. Yet it seemed to him sad that the fire should have quite died down, leaving him inert, a man without impulses. Sometimes he wondered whether he were dead already, until a transient pleasure recalled him to life. His days were pleasant; even this particular day was pleasant.

That's an ineffably sad insight. George is well into his retirement years and as they've been passing, this awful inertia has been insinuating itself into his living. Some days are good, better than others, there are moments. But what is underlying his progress through the relentlessly advancing years is a kind of general frailty.

It's not physical weakness. Old old age is marked with a range of bodily shortcomings, being hard of hearing, having difficulty getting out of a chair, worrying about one's sense of balance. But often frailties are of greater moment.

Brookner appears to have access to the inner worlds of the elderly: maybe it's because she spent her domestic life looking after her own ageing parents. In another novel, *The Next Big Thing*, one of her characters, Julius, has been in conversation with his solicitor and he's been prompted to recall past relationships. He wonders what happened to his late mother's friend, Bijou:

> How had she lived, poor Bijou? And when had she died? There had been no notice in the Deaths column of *The Times*, although there was no reason why there should have been. It had been an obscure life, dignified by a sort of loyalty. That was what he missed, the sort of loyalty observed by people who had little in common but their origins, but who understood each other in a more rooted way than the rootless young could ever understand. He understood it now, almost wished those lost connections back again. He was not trained for freedom, that was the problem, had not been brought up for it. He had done nothing more than glimpse it. The irony was that he now possessed freedom in abundance, but did not quite know how to accommodate it. And it was, it seemed, too late for him to learn.

The riddle to him to solve, the riddle to many ageing people, is how to cope with new-found freedom, not having been brought up for it. Many of the old and the old old have lived consuming, fulfilling lives and now that kind of existence has been taken away from them, they don't know how to adjust and adapt. Julius is afraid he'll never manage.

As with George, a transient pleasure can recall one to life. There are times when I feel good in a supermarket aisle or washing the dishes or driving home from an afternoon screening at the cinema. Nevertheless I have to live with aspects of ageing that make me anxious. I've been fossicking about in a search for a word that expresses this anxiety and I thought for a while it was the word 'brittle'. But that's only part of this syndrome, this collection of symptoms. I have to cope with uncertainty, I am sometimes bewildered (though I used not to be) by choices I have to make. I am therefore indecisive, which leads me to timidity and insecurity. In a word (I think this is the word) I am unsettled in myself.

In an attempt to exert control over my increasingly worrying world, I've become obsessive about what are only minor things: I insist on the toilet rolls being placed in the wall fixture facing outwards; I spend half an hour a week checking the daily/weekly medications for my wife and myself; I tend to regular payment of accounts for gas, electricity and the like with the assiduousness and diligence of the finance manager of a large corporation. Check. Cheque. Check.

I was the only white man invited by a corroboree boss to a four-day circumcision ceremony in the Western Desert. In the 1950s I went with my young wife and a three-month-old baby to England with no job in prospect. I had then no fear. Now I am often consumed by fears. I don't like driving at night or even driving to places I've never been to before. Using my photocopier makes me nervous; what if it jams? The whole technology thing is stressful, the computer, the iPad, Skype, even playing a DVD.

Feeling unsettled like this leads to other markers of ageing. There's forgetfulness of the kind that I have already referred to. Of course such forgetfulness is not only a characteristic of old old age but it goes on being discomforting. Why can't I remember things the way I used to be able to? Is it my brain? Is it a sign that I'm losing the capacity to remember anything? So I make lists of things I have to do and tick them off when they are done. Then I forget to make a list for a sally to the shops and I return with two items not dealt with.

This kind of vagueness is a hallmark of ageing. In its extreme form it leads to incidents that in retrospect are harmlessly amusing (or sometimes seriously distressing). In *Coda*, Thea Astley tells of the life of Kathleen, who becomes an unwelcome burden to her son Brian (called Brain) and daughter Shamrock (called Sham). After yet another incident in which Kathleen gets lost and has to be rescued, Brain worries about her behaviour:

> Was she more difficult than vague? Was that it? Sometimes, he had to concede, she was sharp as a tack. As far as he knew she coped with being alone, still managed with reading, the garden, getting to the shops. He didn't want to admit she needed companionship, fought that admission when that was the one thing, he was beginning to realise, he could possibly do without.
>
> A small history of forgetfulness started. She was locked after hours in a gallery, a cemetery, two large city stores,

and overslept in several cinemas. 'She talks to herself
a lot,' Sham had replied to his concerned phone calls.
'I've heard her out in the yard admonishing plants. God,
Brain, I can't handle it.'

Beaten. He was forced to yield.

'She's bloody lonely,' he said. 'You could do something
about that.'

'So could you,' snapped his sister tartly.

Coda is a satirical novel and in its humorous exaggera-
tions makes its points: there is a seriousness in this extract.
Yes, the elderly do wander off and cause great worry and
inconvenience to their families but here Brain points to the
deep-seated cause: his mother is 'bloody lonely'. Loneliness
(of differing kinds) is a deep-seated element in ageing that
we'll come to in a later chapter.

My frustration with *my* forgetfulness leads into impatience. It is more than mere irritability. Two decades ago I
could deal with situations going awry without finding myself overly ruffled. Not any more. 'Dear,' my wife says, 'I
can't seem to get the screw-top off this jar. Will you have a
go?' Once upon a time I have tried one thing and then another quite calmly until the task was done. Ask me now and
very soon I'm consumed with impatience because I can't do
this damned simple thing straight off. It's because years and
years of remembrances of solving the little domestic prob-
lems with ease come bubbling to the surface, telling me that
I can't do these things any more, that I'm not up to it any

more and of course I get impatient. What's the matter with me? I ask myself. And I know the answer. I'm not up to it any more.

And impatience leads me finally to anger. It's easy to get angry when you're old. Things are never what they used to be. Anger is always an element in the caricature of old age. Old old people are regularly portrayed as grumpy, irascible, tetchy, cranky, ill-tempered, crusty. I know a number who are. It's easy to get or be angry if you're old. Negative though it may be as a personality trait, negative in the sense of impingeing on our relating to others, anger results from explicable experiences or attitudes. It may be at the bottom of deep sorrow or disappointment; it may result from ongoing pain or myriad physical frustrations; it may have its origins in loneliness or a deep fear of what the future may bring. It comes from that understandable but psychologically inappropriate question: why me?

In an attempt to wrestle some sense out of our obsessions and fears, our impatience and our anger, we go on looking in other people's lives for something to sustain us. Philip Roth's novel, *Everyman*, is essentially about someone who has become what he does not want to be. The Everyman figure has no name but, like the mediaeval Everyman, he really does stand for all of us. This Everyman is well into his ageing and in a period of loneliness, having seen an obituary notice for a former colleague, rings the widow, Gwen, to offer condolences.

'Was it a stroke or was it a heart attack?' he asked her.

'It was a myocardial infarct.'

'Had he been feeling ill?'

'Well, his blood pressure had been – well, he had a lot of trouble with his blood pressure. And then this past weekend he wasn't feeling so great. His blood pressure had gone up again.'

'They couldn't control that with drugs?'

'They did. He took all kinds of drugs. But he probably had a lot of arterial damage. You know, bad old arteries, and there's a point at which the body wears out. And he was so weary at that point. He said to me just a couple of nights ago, "I'm so weary". He wanted to live, but there wasn't anything anybody could do to keep him alive any longer. Old age is a battle, dear, if not with this, then with that. It's an unrelenting battle, and just when you're at your weakest and least able to call up your old fight.'

After the call to Gwen Everyman felt the need to contact some others of his former colleagues, and it was not easy. In each of three calls he made there was

the predictable banality and futility of the pep talk …
the attempt to revive the old esprit by reviving memories
of his colleagues' lives, by trying to find things to say
to buck up the hopeless and bring them back from the
brink –

For hours after he'd put the phone down, he found himself reflecting on Gwen's 'unrelenting battle':

> Had he been aware of the mortal suffering of every man and woman he happened to have known during all his years of professional life, of each one's painful story of regret and loss and stoicism, of fear and panic and isolation and dread, had he learned of every last thing they had parted with that had once been vitally theirs and of how, systematically, they were being destroyed, he would have had to stay on the phone through the day and into the night, making another hundred calls at least. Old age isn't a battle; old age is a massacre.

There's too much anger here for me. It's not that I can't empathise with his bitterness and his grim resentment. I understand how hard it is to find things to say 'to buck up the hopeless'. I've heard a dear and elderly friend in pain say to me, 'I just want to die. I can't deal with things any more. If only it would all come to an end.' And what *is* there to say?

But anger doesn't seem to be a helpful answer. I have first-hand experience here. Following my open heart surgery I was subject to a regime of medications which lasted month after month. We scarcely now even pay attention to newspaper and television reports of young people whose dangerous behaviour has been caused by mind-altering drugs. Even drugs legally administered can play with the brain. It depends on the individual's metabolism and also the crossover effect of other drugs being taken at the same time. Some months into my recuperation first my wife and then my three children all noted that I was becoming irascible and short-tempered. Not my way of being at all, they agreed. I had changed. I had become an angry old man. Aware that becoming dependent on Google for medical opinion was ill-advised, my wife nevertheless checked the Internet for possible side-effects of my drugs and there she found what she and the family had suspected: one of the drugs had caused in me what we could only call a personality change. Reducing the dosage of the offending drug almost magically returned me to my old self.

But the point of this anecdote is not medical. It demonstrates the corrosive effect of anger, for my human relationships during that period became fractured. My own angry responses caused sharp responses in others ('What's the matter with Ian?'). If anger is a risk in old old age, it's a risk not worth taking. It leads to an unending bleakness.

A former colleague of mine lived apparently comfortably into his 90s. I'd always thought of him like a coiled spring; pleasant and charming in social intercourse though he was, I sensed something burning in him. However, in retirement, he settled into a strict routine, 9:30 am into his workshop (he was an accomplished woodworker), lunch at 12:45, a glass of sherry at 5 pm, bed at 9:30. I found it suffocating to observe. His son, however, put his finger on an explanation of this rigour, when he said to me, 'Dad's been waiting half his life to be old; he loves it.' Sitting in a chair dozing, indolently pottering about the house or garden, idling through the days promises a kind of safety and comfort.

The frailties of old old age are assumed to be physical. That's why we take a stick when walking, or check the gas isn't on before going out, or hold onto the banister coming down stairs. We look to be safe and at ease, to mitigate things like our forgetfulness and impatience. But the physical is that immediate part of our being that we attend to: if we don't, our bodies quickly remind us to be attentive. There is, however, what goes on in our heads.

There are frailties there, like not being able to remember things or getting things muddled or finding ourselves cranky for no good reason. What is concerning is that we ignore our capacity as we age for reflecting, for speculating. Probably when we were in our 60s it occurred to us that there were dangers in only reading what we agreed with and the dangers increase into our old old age. The phrase 'set in their ways' applies not only to physical behaviours but also to ways of thinking. We do feel safe reading about issues we agree with; that sort of reading is a comfort. A friend of mine, older than I am, has for some time been rereading from his past *Adam Bede*, *The Mayor of Casterbridge*, *Moby Dick* and *Middlemarch*. He has, he said, loved reading them again and I can understand his pleasure, but it's a temperament thing. I don't do it. I think there's so much going on that I'd rather try something new to me, contemporary American writers, debut Australian novels. In them I live in the attitudes of now. Not that they all please or comfort me. Often they annoy me: they're far too long (900 pages is a marathon) or too smug or too self-obsessed, but at least they help me feel that I'm still living in the world. I need that feeling because weariness, fragility, sorrow and a whole constellation of disappointments will, if I don't do anything about it, narrow my final years into a gloomy windowless cell that has clanged shut on me. That's why I look for interesting movies or check out presenters on the Internet's TED Talks. I've got to stop myself from wearing daggy clothes and staring into space from an armchair.

I feel so sad for non-readers of my age. So much is denied them. And it occurs to me that because of the all-pervasiveness of the Internet, current octogenarians will be one of the last generations to indulge in deep reading. I feel so sad for those who suffer from Parkinson's or onset dementia or failing eyesight, those who can't read even though they thought they wanted to. These reflections of mine won't make it to the consciousness of those people, anyway. I'm trying to address the fortunate in old old age who keep teetering on the edge of giving up life too early.

– 6 –

Intimacy

In old old age we sometimes revisit our own childhoods, searching for meaning in ways in which later generations don't. In his mid-20s my father had slogged with his infantry battalion through the mud of the Somme, endured the horrendous noise of artillery, the cries of his wounded mates, but of all this he never spoke, ever. I only knew him as an inward parent and there must have been thousands of fathers like him. He was carrying anyway an inheritance from the Victorian era of familial distance, and the war and the Depression only added to it. James McAuley got it so right in his poem 'Because':

> *My father and my mother never quarrelled.*
> *They were united in a kind of love*
> *As daily as the* Sydney Morning Herald
> *Rather than like the eagle or the dove.*

I never saw them casually touch,
Or show a moment's joy in one another.
Why should this matter to me now so much?

It matters to me because my wife and I have been able to show joy in one another and I want to know how this has come about. I was the only child to survive three pregnancies and that was a burden I carried until my parents were both dead. With my undemonstrative father and sweet, thoughtful mother I grew up in a silent household. I never felt lonely because I was a solitary creature, but there was a later decade with a cheerful and bouncy stepmother which enabled me to have a youth marked with fun and friends. I was able to counter the silence I had known. I now wonder whether the sociologists are right when they suggest that in old age who we are remains pretty close to what we were when we were young.

I can remember, up the unfrequented sideway of two of the houses we lived in, setting up a battlefield for my toy soldiers and a farm for my toy animals. I never invited any of my friends to see what I had done. Actually, I didn't have many friends: I found my own company quite satisfying. When I was immobilised by polio I read a lot. It was the only way I could feel part of the world and reading for me became a lifelong habit; I would read anything, the back of a cereal packet or an advertisement on a bus. Another solitary activity for me was collecting. Of course I collected postage stamps (didn't all boys?), but I also avidly collected cards of cricketers, footballers and kings and queens of England. In my old old age I have collections, two of them. I have over the years put together a modest collection of Persian rugs, ranging from a small Quchan prayer rug to a large Gabbeh. I also have several shelves of books on the Victorian period of history, from a number of biographies of Queen Victoria herself to a collection of letters between a Norfolk vicar and his squire. I still read incessantly, anything, travel, literary fiction, essays. I don't have a lot of intimate friends and am content in my own company. If I'm honest, there's a kind of revisiting of the silent household atmosphere of my childhood. I live in my head. My wife is constantly asking me, 'What are you thinking? What's going on in your brain? Tell me.'

People in old old age fall into several categories: there are those who remain single all their lives for a variety of reasons; there are those who have lost their partners and are long-term or recent widows or widowers; there are those whose marriages have broken down and haven't wanted to risk another close relationship; there are those who have been married but are childless; there are those where one is frail and the other is the carer; there are those who have had children from a marriage that has maintained its course. Each of these situations has its own structure and mode of being. Because I've been part of a married relationship for over 60 years, that's the only one relationship I can reflect upon with any confidence. I have friends and acquaintances who belong in other categories and I think I can imagine how they address their circumstances, but I am a husband, father, grandfather, and great-grandfather and that's it.

When I was in my late teens and early 20s, like all the age-peers I knew, I mixed in with the local community. There weren't all that many of us who had a car or a motorbike and travel outside our own suburb was not easy. Not everybody had a telephone, even. Our friendship groups came from school, or church, or sports teams like netball, tennis, cricket; there we met our friends' sisters and brothers at social gatherings. There we met our first boyfriend or girlfriend, and these early relationships were comparatively easy to foster. We had so much in common, we lived within walking or cycling reach of each other. Often our parents knew each other. We belonged in the same suburb and therefore more or less shared a common social class. How easy was all that?

When, therefore, old old agers come to talk with their grandchildren about relationships with the opposite sex, the conversational terrain is uneven. Our grandchildren met their partners in pubs several suburbs from where they live, or by chance at a concert, or on a train: race, colour, or ethnicity is never an issue. And this is only one of a vast range of topics that younger generations often avoid with the elderly. For their own part, the elderly find themselves victims of a worldview that concentrates attention on the future, on what's next on the agenda. There is little or no awareness that that now has succeeded a past and that past is of any account. When, therefore, the old old agers talk about when *they* were young, the millennials especially tune out: the past is gone and with it its meaning.

The people of my generation are tempted to say it like it was, and when they do, they alienate the young. In Anne Tyler's recent Man Booker shortlisted *A Spool of Blue Thread*, the elderly Junior Whitshank has gathered his family for dinner and is making critical remarks to children and grandchildren alike. Around the table there is an unease:

> How could this man have been the hero of Mrs. Whitshank's romance? Whether you found it dashing or tawdry, at least it *had* been a romance, complete with intrigue and scandal and a wrenching separation. But Junior Whitshank was dry as a bone, droning on relentlessly while the other diners ate their food in dogged silence. Only his wife was looking at him, her face alight with interest as he discussed the value of hard labor, then the deplorable lack of initiative in the younger generation, then the benefits conferred by having lived through the Great Depression. If young folks today had lived through a depression the way *he* had lived through a depression –

The younger generation were aware of Junior Whitshank's sermonising, were used to it. They've been told before that they have no drive, that if only they'd been through the Depression like Junior, they would be far better fitted for life. And as the family members briefly glanced up at their boring eldest, they found themselves wondering how Linnie Mae had ever found him a romantic hero. For here she was, gazing adoringly at him as he berated his family for what he saw as their shiftlessness.

Parents get a bad press from their children. Never does it occur to them that their parents ever kissed under a suburban streetlight, or sat on a hilltop together holding hands and watched the sunset. I think our three children wonder how our marriage has lasted so long.

Dorothy and I are first of all temperamentally different. She enjoys people in a way I don't: she loves conversation. She manages old age far better than I do. With her arthritis and my polio knee we can't go on walks together as we used to. All our married life until the last 10 years we walked together, along country roads, through forests, by riverbanks, around suburban streets; by the hour we walked. It's now lost to us but Dorothy has dealt with the loss better than I have.

She has an ongoing loyalty to her friends and spends much time on the phone talking to them. She remembers the names of all their children and grandchildren just as she remembers the phone numbers of all those people she calls or who call her. She is an interesting friend and to me she's never mentally bored. She amasses a wide range of factual and imaginative information and reflective ideas from her iPad and reading. Sometimes she aches all over but maintains an inner vitality. She is impatient with her physical body and that's not helped by my solitariness. Therefore we have to make constant adjustments in our marriage in order to maintain our friendship.

This friendship is in old age instrumental. That is, it majors on helpfulness. I will fetch things for her, her sewing box or a nail file to save her getting up onto her painful knee. She will read out to me an article from the newspaper that I missed and comment on it. We share kitchen and laundry chores. It's a very poor exchange, that I get her breakfast in bed and cups of coffee for us and the predinner nibbles and gin and tonics, while she (a very imaginative cook) gets lunches and always restaurant-style evening meals.

As a male old old ager I can feel guilty about our relationship because Dorothy is dealing with ageing better than I am. And I don't think this is just Dorothy. I think it's true of all women. They deal better with the difficulties of old age than men. Elderly women can handle loneliness better than men. When I observe my female age-peers I find they probably have a stronger hold on their youth. The consuming bread-winning years in a man's life for my generation often tend to give him a notion that he is in control of his world, but in old age the feeling that he's obsolete, as it were, affects the way he deals with life. He has become 'elderly': he feels old. He doesn't care as much about his appearance as he used to, and certainly not as women do about theirs.

Ageing women (they live on average five years longer than men) are more sociable with each other. Men share activities; women share feelings. They thrive on building and nourishing friendships. Men's friendships are less intimate and supportive than women's. Women reach out to each other in a way that men don't or cannot. When I came to look for an explanation of this sex difference, I first thought it had to do with feminine nurture, that women were hard-wired, in a way men weren't, to care for others and show an ongoing empathy. Now I'm not so sure. There may be another factor in play here.

Men of my generation almost universally expected (it was the late 1940s and early 1950s) to leave school, find a job, perhaps study, and stay in that career until they retired. With women, a series of transitions marked their lives. Most women left school and went to work, then got married and became (in my generation) housewives who stayed at home to clean and cook meals. Then they had children and dealt with maternal responsibilities. Then the children grew up and left home and the woman's role changed yet again. She perhaps rejoined the workforce. Women had become accustomed to change and impermanence. When, therefore, old age and old old age came upon them, most dealt with this new stage as just another transition in their lives. To adopt once again a new role and way of being was relatively easy for women. Their men had had an uninterrupted linear progress through the years, while they were used to coping with change. Their consequent flexibility allows them to meet advancing years with an equanimity not given to men.

Such is the situation with me and Dorothy. She copes with our ageing far better than I do. I get cranky with my physical frailties, especially when they prevent me from with ease doing stuff like putting on a Band-Aid or tying up a parcel. She calms me down, and tells me it's not important, not worth making a fuss about. When she complains about an aching shoulder and I offer sympathy, she tells me it's not a big deal. That's the difference. And the difference is what enables us to cope with frailty.

Members of the Whitshank family were at least able to believe that their parents had once had a romantic relationship. To believe it now was for them another matter altogether. Many if not most of the children of the elderly likewise find it hard to imagine that their ageing parents have any romance left in their lives.

When I first had the idea of putting together some thoughts on how old old age was affecting me, I made a collection of newspaper and magazine cuttings which purported to be about elderly behaviours. One of the categories in my cuttings was the issue of sexual relations. Firstly, the journalists penning these pieces seem to feel they were required to write on the edge of surprise. One headline read, 'The Sex Gets Better'; another read, 'Did the rocking chair move for you?' Secondly, the couples interviewed seemed predominantly to be in their middle to late 50s. The oldest surveyed were into the mid to late 70s. So is that when sex ends? At the old age of 78 or so?

I don't intend to set down an exposé of my sex life but it seems proper to explore the possibilities that remain into old old age. Of course through the late 60s and the 70s there is a decline in physical ardour as there is a decline in physical activities like tennis or house painting. However, physical desire never fades entirely in an intimate relationship that has lasted 60 years or more. I can look across our living room, see Dorothy in conversation with a friend and my heart (yes, still) skips a beat. There are here two things operating: I hear her voice and its inflections and I'm reminded of the enduring nature of our friendship. This is someone I know and love and who knows and loves me and seeing her gives me great comfort but also my eye takes in the cut of her hair and the gestures of her hands, the shift of her body as she crosses her legs, and I am reminded of the countless times we have had urgent yet loving sexual encounters. We are sometimes together totally unprepared for the way our years of relating call us to intimacy. When that happens we both feel cherished.

Openness to intimacy has a temporal element to it. By this I mean that intimacy has to do with the when-ness of our view of the world. For us octogenarians the future has long begun to shrink: in some senses it's scarcely a when at all that we can look forward to. We are thrown back onto the past: lots of when there. What's left is the present; it's after all where we do our living.

But living in the present isn't easy for some people. They are afraid of it, even. In the middle of last century, the British comedienne, Joyce Grenfell, offered a prayer: 'There is only this minute, Lord, and I'm in it'. There's a wealth of wisdom in that. What have we really got but the now? Instinct tells us that life can't get any more real than now. But what if our here and now is somehow lacking, disappointing, unfair, difficult? We shy away from it, thinking there's something better somewhere, in the past, maybe. Philosopher Henry David Thoreau put it like this:

> You must live in the present, launch yourself on every wave, find your eternity in each moment. Fools stand on their island of opportunities and look toward another land. There is no other land; there is no other life but this.

The most intimate thing we can do for ourselves is to learn to live 'in the present'. I commented earlier about a cheerful greeting from a shopkeeper and how refreshing I found it: that was an experience from 'this minute' and I was 'in it'!

In the next chapter we shall consider among other things the value of a community for the old old. For now, it seems appropriate to think about ways that may enhance the shift from the now into the possibility of meaningful relating. All I'm doing here is suggesting a useful exercise to facilitate openness. I have in mind a group of six or so friends who could meet for a coffee morning or a cheese and wine evening, nothing formal. Two little books are involved for whoever calls the group together. One is Theodor Zeldin, *Conversation: How Talk Can Change Your Life*, Harvill Press, London, 1998, which has chapter headings like 'What saves family conversation from being boring' and 'How conversation encourages the meeting of minds'. The other is Evelyn McFarlane and James Saywell, *If ... Ques-*

tions for the Game of Life, Hodder and Stoughton, London 1995 with 500 questions like 'If you were to select the food that best describes your character, what food would it be?' and 'If you had to choose the single most valuable thing you ever learned, what would it be?'

If the members of the group are living in the now and paying close attention, intimate attitudes and responses may well be revelatory and encompassing.

– 7 –

Family and Others

Dorothy and I rather foolishly thought that *we* would bring up our three children. Up to a point this was true. We encouraged them to become involved with the Argonauts, that ABC radio club; they entered writing and drawing competitions. We always insisted we sat down together at meal times; regularly we had what we called 'reading teas', when everybody brought to the table whatever they happened to be reading and read it without interruption during the meal. Violin and clarinet lessons were part of every week for the children. We did what we could to let them see that helpfulness and thoughtfulness towards others was an important part of growing up. As parents, it had never occurred to us that at some later stage we would be elderly, or to the children. Together we played Monopoly and card games, went on long Sunday walks with the dog. We romped in the back garden, spent days at the beach. We went camping and exploring rough tracks in the bush. I think we were lively parents. Then came the 70s.

This was a decade like no other. It began with the publication of Germaine Greer's *The Female Eunuch*. Then the subversive *Little Red Schoolbook* came to Australia to the consternation of many. In 1972 the world was aghast at the massacre of Israeli athletes at the Munich Olympic Games. The following year saw in Australia the advent of *Countdown*, the must-see programme of pop music for teenagers to scream at, while on the other side of the world there was the spectacle of America's President Nixon and the Watergate scandal. In 1973 Patrick White was awarded the Nobel Prize for literature. 1975 saw at home the dismissal of the Whitlam government and news came of mass atrocities in Cambodia. Vietnamese asylum seekers began to arrive on Australian shores in their thousands. The world mourned the death of Elvis Presley. These were tumultuous years and our children lived their teens through them all.

Small wonder that a kind of universal restlessness and even horror had an effect on young people in relatively relaxed Australia. It threw the calm they had known into turmoil. They heard a call to independence and a throwing-off of domestic restraints. Thus it was that the children of middle-class old old agers left school at the end of Year 12 and many left home. They went into residence in university colleges or into shared housing. They saw fleeing the nest as a rite of passage. There were consequences. In their late teens they were suddenly free. There were no regular mealtimes or bed-time. There were no checks on changing socks or cleaning teeth. Significantly there were no adult voices. The only voices they heard were their own.

This suddenly free generation saw little of their parents. Of course they rang up (weekly?) to 'check in' and came home for a meal from time to time with a load of washing or a fractured relationship to bemoan. But the daily ritual of the family's evening meal was gone; the older adult alternative position on matters was more and more rarely heard, nor did these flying visitors take in encouragement and praise from caring parents. So it came about that the children of parents in their 40s had only tenuous ties to those parents. By the time that the children had earned qualifications and had steady employment, they had developed a new set of friends and acquaintances and had adjusted to their independence. Now in their mid-20s their need for parental support and guidance had faded. What they remembered about their parents was a couple in their prime, full of energy, apparently self-sufficient. Nothing to worry about there. We can just get on with our lives.

And over the next forty years they did. They married and had children, they moved house, they got divorced, they changed careers. Yet always at the backs of their minds they maintained an image of their parents as being lively, resourceful, ever-youthful and stable. When I last lived with them, that's what they were like.

And the children, therefore, cannot imagine that their parents could possibly have changed in any way. In an obviously autobiographical short story, 'After Long Absence', Janette Turner Hospital tells of an expatriate academic author who is returning home to Brisbane to lecture and she is staying with her ageing parents. She was brought up in a fundamentalist/literalist Bible-believing Christian family, caring, generous, loving. However, the writer found this religious style didn't sit easily in her academic milieu. She was in fact dreading meeting her parents after a long absence. By letter over some years she has persuaded her father to enrol in a university course and it occurred to her that it would give him pleasure to have lunch with her academic colleagues in the University's staff club lounge. Her father is delighted and secretly flattered.

> At the table reserved for us the waiter is asking, 'red or white, sir?' and my heart sinks. The air is full of greeting and reminiscence, but I am waiting for my father's inevitable gesture … I am bracing myself to stay calm, knowing I will be as angered by the small patronizing smiles of my old friends as by my father's compulsion to 'bear witness'. He will turn his wineglass upside down at the very least; possibly he will make some mild moral comment on drink; he may offer the peace that passeth understanding to the staff club at large.
>
> He does none of these things.
>
> To my astonishment, he permits the waiter to fill his glass with white wine. He is bemused, I decide, by his surroundings. And yet twice during the course of the meal, he takes polite sips from his glass.

The magnitude of this gesture overwhelms me. I have to excuse myself from the table for ten minutes.

Adult children find it difficult to accept that their parents can change. Their parents are often more alert to situations and people's needs than their children give them credit for. That, for ageing parents, is a frustration. The visiting lecturer's father makes a gesture that comes from deep wisdom and awareness. Now their parents have entered old old age, children still want to believe that nothing has changed. 'Mum and dad will be fine', they say. But it is so difficult to persuade them that we are *not* fine. Not all the time, at least. We need comfort, we need concern being shown, we need understanding. We are old. Old. This isn't the cry of grumpy cranky old men and women. I'm not being critical of my children whom I love dearly and know they love Dorothy and me dearly. They are simply part of a particular generation. I talk with my age-peers and I hear the same story: they wish they saw more of their children or heard from them more often. Dorothy's 80th birthday was a great occasion: everybody had a great time. But we don't want great occasions. We just want regular and frequent phone calls, postcards from them. Nothing extravagant or lengthy. I know our children try. I know my friends' children try. But aren't we allowed to be a little greedy for company in our old age? Maybe we brought it on ourselves. Maybe we tried too hard not to be a burden to our children, especially when they were, are at their peak in occupational responsibilities or with their own demanding children.

Kate Llewellyn is an author with a wide range, poet, essayist, travel writer and diarist. Her journals give account of her gardening experiences and in *A Fig at the Gate* she describes in detail a pair of sparrows feeding their young in an afternoon of fierce temperatures.

> Is it oxytocin that keeps the pair feeding their young hour after hour in the heat? Perhaps they have nested there for seasons. It is unusual to have this heat in November so this is an arduous time for the birds. Oxytocin, that powerful chemical which keeps us devoted to our children and, sometimes, to others not so suited. And it is an irony I find amusing that while adult children have it for their own children, they do not have it for their parents. That is nature. Jane recently quoted another friend who said, 'I'd like to get my hands on the person who said that your children will be a comfort in your old age.' No, I'm not meaning my own children, only that I see how connected we are to sparrows.

Parenthood is a vexed issue. Our eldest child (strange to use the word 'child') is into his 60s; he is getting to be young-old. Yet we still worry for him, as we worry for all of our children. Is it oxytocin? And what about nature? We go on feeding them. Do they feed us?

Remember Mrs Palfrey, the elderly widow who was finding the simple act of walking something of a challenge? Here she is again, reflecting still on the issue of freedom:

Sometimes, when I was a young, married woman, I longed to be freed – free of nursery chores and social obligations, one's duty, d'you know? And free of worries, too, about one's loved ones – childish ailments and ageing parents, money troubles, everyone at times feels the longing – to run away from it all. But it's really not to be desired – and I realise that's the only *way* of being free – to be not needed … My daughter no longer needs me – indeed, her dread is that it might one day be the other way about.

She is right, of course. We want to be not needed. We want that freedom. But there's the rub. What we have to pay to be free is not seeing our children as often as we would like.

A newspaper report has told of Chinese regulations designed to ensure that adult children visit their parents or phone them regularly. Failure to do so may incur financial penalties in the form of lowered credit ratings. Regulations in Shanghai compel children to 'visit and send greetings often' to their elderly parents; parents older than 60 are to be visited 'frequently'. Under these laws parents can take their children to court for failure to give them emotional and practical support. Such insistence on caring for the elderly is certainly not new in Chinese society: it was common as far back as 900 years. Of course my age-peers and I have no such expectations of our adult children, but the very idea itself has a wistfulness about it.

In the late 1980s Alan Bennett wrote for television a series of half a dozen monologues under the title *Talking*

Heads (Bennett himself played one of the characters). The monologue-portraits range from elderly Doris to a young vicar's wife, Suzanne. One of the very touching characterisations was entitled 'Soldiering On'. It pictures Muriel, a middle-class widow, who constantly fortifies herself with helpful cliches. She believes her wealthy husband has left her very well provided for but her son, Giles, takes over her financial affairs and in looking to profit himself from that income begins to lose it all. Muriel has to watch her large house and possessions sold, she has to leave a retirement home because it becomes too expensive and it's all to do with Giles's mismanagement of the family's finances. Eventually Muriel finds for herself a room in a seaside boarding house:

> Been here about a month now. Got onto it via an advert in *The Lady*. Sledmere it's called, 'Holiday flatlets'. Off-season, of course, and quite reasonable. I haven't quite got the town sorted out yet. I feel sure there must be a community here if only I can put my finger on it. I had a word with a young woman at the Town Hall. Blue fingernails but civil enough otherwise. Said was I interested in Meals on Wheels. I said, 'Rather. I was 2 i/c Meals on Wheels for the whole of Sudbury,' a fund of experience. Brawn not too good but brains available to be picked at any time. She looked a bit blank. Turns out she meant did I want to be on the receiving end. I said, 'Not on your life.' But message received and understood. The old girl's past it…
>
> Don't see [Giles] and Pippa much, not a peep out of

them for over a month now. Doesn't like to come down, says it upsets him. Don't know why. Doesn't upset me. Miss the tinies. Not so tiny, Lucy'll be twelve now. And twelve is like fifteen. Married next. I'd seen myself as a model grandmother, taking them to Peter Pan and the Science Museum. Not to be. Another dream bites the dust.

Many elderlies, especially those in their 80s, can feel discarded, abandoned. They probably had a part-sentimental and romantic notion that their old age would find them surrounded by family and friends, having lively conversations, almost basking in love and affection. Invitations to concerts or bridge parties or golf would come weekly and there would be so much in their lives that was fulfilling. But these experiences-to-be often become a fantasy. One after another the dreams bit the dust, to be replaced by a dull and seemingly bottomless loneliness. No one wants this for oneself or for that matter for anyone else. As for Muriel, she misses most in the family the teenage Crispin and Lucy.

In many or most families there is this third generation – grandchildren. Grandchildren are an interesting group, our representatives of ongoing inheritance. For example, my wife's mother was a highly competent seamstress but Dorothy was hopeless at sewing and had no interest in it. However, our daughter is a skilled dressmaker and can produce with flair ranges of costumes for school plays she directs. Skills like these (and attitudes, too) can skip a generation. Dorothy is a musician of great skill, perfect pitch and all that, but our three children, while sympathetic to music of all kinds, never would have seen themselves as musicians. Yet Dorothy has a grandson who is musical, as she is, and who works as a sound engineer for a recording company: a generation skip again.

Five of our grandchildren we saw little of as they were growing up because they lived interstate. Two, a brother and a sister, we were able to spend time with, however, well into their 20s, and we established a relationship that is both frank and tender. For old old agers to have such a closeness with a younger generation is refreshing. I'm not sure what we do for *them* but we are certainly aware of what they do for *us*. I don't only mean helping us to negotiate the (to us) confusing world of IT, like buying online or booking airfares: I mean they brighten our days. A favourite negro spiritual of mine has the words, 'My life's cloudy, send dem angels down'; grandchildren can be those angels. One of ours lives and works in London and Skypes us often for no particular reason. The other lives two suburbs away and also for no particular reason will ring to check if it's okay for him, as he puts it, 'to swing by' and see us. I think this caring for us had to do with the fact that he and his sister had been able to observe us ageing in the way in which our children couldn't. They are aware of our frailties: 'You stay there, Gran'ma. I'll get it for you' and 'We are not going until we have done the dishes'. We were talking about this matter once when the grandson's wife said, with a smile, 'They say, don't they, grandchildren get on better with their grandparents because they have a common enemy!' That's a bit harsh, but it trails some truth with it. None of this has anything to do with love. It's a social issue, the result of shifting dynamics in relationships, and there's no denying it.

There's another 'they say, don't they' that touches on our affinity with others: 'Friends are God's apology for relations'. Sociologists tell us that in a lifetime we gain five close friends and fifteen good friends. By the time we've reached our 80s we tend to have lost some of these friends. My oldest close friend (from childhood, actually) has died and several of my good friends have also died. My surviving friends date from about fifty years and more ago and they are important to me as I age. They are representatives of the past I knew and thought I understood; they are a comfort to me. I feel at ease in their company and free to disagree with them, to join in their complaints, to occasionally weep but more often laugh about the state of the world. I do have a problem and Dorothy reminds me of it often. She quotes at me Dr Johnson's wise observation, 'A man, sir, should keep his friendships in good repair'. I'm not good at that. I try to excuse it by telling myself that it stems from my being an only child; I don't have the need for intimacy with others. However, some remarkable chemistry has meant that these friends have held onto me. Sitting down with pen and paper, I can make a list of more than five intimate friends and more than fifteen good friends and for that I'm eternally grateful to them.

The wonderful thing about the friendship issue is that it is not dependent on a long period of relating. From retirement age and on, one can develop friendships that are new but soon seem old. In my 80s I became friends with two, perhaps three people I never knew before. I guess it was just being open to possibilities.

There is a caricature abroad of the old elderly who withdraw into some hiding-place they find cosy and seldom venture out. I know several people like that. It is such a dangerous ploy. Whatever the current public manifestation of change, we are tribal beings. Beyond familial bounds there is a social and sociable ring of personal connections that enhances and enlarges our experience of living. If as we age, we ignore that outer ring, we are diminished. We cannot afford to shrink from community, because we need a context within which to find friends. This need explains the rise in the number of Men's Sheds across the country. As we've already observed, women deal better with ageing than men: it's men who need a structured meeting place, like a workshop for hobbies. Acquaintances tell me that their Men's Shed experiences are positive, that they get to meet other men across common interests. Several of them have told me how casual meetings have developed into intimacy, that they have found someone to talk to, even to depend upon and enjoy.

The same sense of community can be found for men and women alike in meeting within new movements like U3A and Probus. Friendships developed in such groups tend to begin as special interest relationships, from French conversation classes or music history sessions, but may become more intimate over time. As we noted in the second chapter of this little guide, old old agers grew through childhood and into their teens in a predominantly churchgoing society. In my case churchgoing was not negotiable; my father was a theologically liberal nonconformist clergyman and it never occurred to him or to me that I wouldn't regularly attend church services and functions. Church congregations became my communities. In those communities I met a wide range of age-peers and older people, a crane driver, a newspaper editor, a factory manager, a dressmaker, a carpenter, a jazz pianist, a hospital matron, a trucking magnate. From childhood to my current old old age, my community outside educational institutions was the church. And still is.

That I'm a churchgoer is only another way of saying I belong to an encompassing community. Putting aside the details of the belief system that underpins churchgoing, it provides me with the milieu where I interact with people who have a commonality. I engage in worship and spiritual reflection but within this community I also discuss social issues, gossip about football, share gardening tips, express sympathy and wonderment, feel comfort and a belongingness. With these people I am able to further explore areas in my search for optimism. I go to church and engage in what we might call spiritual exercises and then over a cup of tea or coffee I am caught up in an exchange of views or hopes or memories or moral puzzles that leave me refreshed. I come away from this immersion in community feeling grateful for the experience. Simply put, that is one of the principal functions of community, to encourage in such associating a feeling of inclusion. It's an antidote to loneliness.

Given the convenience of taps on the mobile or clicks with a mouse, one could be forgiven for believing that communicating with people was never easier than now. However, the fact of the matter seems to be that the elderly have never been more lonely: social surveys certainly suggest it.

And novelists, too. In Margaret Drabble's *The Dark Flood Rises*, one of the elderly characters, Theresa, is prey to loneliness:

> Her right hand cradles her mobile phone. She waits for it to bleep or buzz or flash or ring. If only somebody would ring or text, someone, anyone, someone from out there, from the world of the living. Even that false and endlessly repeating recorded message purporting to be from her bank would do. She wills her little gadget to speak to her. It remains silent.
>
> Any sound would rescue her.
>
> Her hands are withered and wrinkled as well as enfeebled, and their backs have for some years now been manifesting the pale-brown liver spots of age. She stares at them, attempting to distract herself. She doesn't dislike these spots. They have a certain charm, even an elegance. She'll miss them when she's dead.

The emptiness of the room in which Theresa is sitting is intense. The world of the living is out of her reach, she feels. She finds herself even taking some desperate pleasure in the liver spots on the backs of her hands.

There are obvious situations where loneliness is almost inevitable: widows and widowers living alone, never married or never partnered individuals. They wake up each morning to a silent house or apartment, they eat breakfast alone, only the radio speaks, or a TV chat panel. They feed the cat or greet the dog. These isolated old old agers somehow cope. They are not without well-meaning advice: they should work at their computer skills, they should engage in conversation with the young people at the supermarket checkout, they should plan their weeks and have something to do or to look forward to every day. The solitary says things like 'I quite enjoy my own company' or 'I've never been terribly sociable'. I once had a neighbour who would have expressed that view. The risk they run is that in their self-imposed isolation they tend to further insulate themselves against social interaction and push people away, which only intensifies their loneliness. Hence the caricature of the elderly recluse seeming to want to avoid human contact. There's a further category of the lonely, which covers the situation of a live-in couple. It's not uncommon among the elderly for one member of a couple (married or partnered) to experience intense loneliness even in the presence of another. Old age, unless dealt with, can have a twisted effect on relationships, even those that once had been intimate.

Not much gets said about loneliness. Many of us live in upbeat Western affluence. Magazines, Facebook, all popular media focus on celebrity, on the rich and famous where everything is exciting and bright, the sun always shines. We are much into celebration and anniversary. To use that wonderful title of Neil Postman's study of public discourse we are *Amusing Ourselves to Death*. We have little time or inclination to give serious consideration of human conditions like being lonely. Maybe loneliness is seen as a precursor to death and we never want to be found even thinking about that. Or maybe it's the pace of life; everybody is in a hurry. Even in speech: why does the speech of millennials especially become so rapid? Why do newsreaders and TV journalists gabble so? Because there's no time.

Certainly no time to contemplate calmly how the world goes. That's for those in their old old age. If they can disengage from precipitate onward rush. If they can free themselves from the inheritance of busyness with people and things.

– 8 –

Mind as Resource

Fleur Adcock is a New Zealand-born poet who has made her considerable reputation in Britain; she emigrated there in 1963. A late collection of her poems (entitled *Glass Wings*) appeared in 2013 on the eve of her 80th birthday. She has a deft touch when writing about old age and one of her poems is called, simply, 'Alumnae Notes'. In it she laments the death of one of her school friends and the descent into dementia of another; the poem closes with

> *The class photos fade. But Marie and I,*
> *face to face on Skype in full colour*
> *and still far too animated to die,*
>
> *can see we've not yet turned to sepia.*

The lines attend to a conundrum of ageing. How are we to behave, to appear, even as we grow older and older?

We can reflect on the lives we have known, on people who have died or are languishing in a nursing home or struggle to survive in an empty house. Or we can meet up with a Marie or a George 'in full colour' on Skype.

Too often the elderly are portrayed as careless about their appearance. If a documentary-filmmaker wants to illustrate a point regarding the old, he or she employs the clip of a couple hobbling along arm in arm dressed in daggy trackie-dacks, bulky cardigans and clumsy Nike joggers, looking uncared for. It doesn't need to be like this. Nothing pleases me more than to hear my grandson say, 'Hey, Gran'ma, I like your new shirt/jumper/jacket'. It's Fleur Adcock saying with her friend Marie, 'we've not yet turned to sepia'.

There's another Antipodean-born poet who's made his reputation in Britain, the Australian, Clive James. He's a better poet than anything else (unless it's in literary criticism). In a poem he calls 'Holding Court', James cleverly describes a gathering in which he himself is the focus. He's too deaf to follow all the nuances of the conversation and can't quite see all the people in the room. Age is weighing heavily on him in his 'waning day' and in his mind, 'the fires are dying fast'. He wonders whether he shouldn't

> Be pleased that things are simple now, at least,
> As certitude succeeds bewilderment.
> The storm blew out and this is the dead calm.
> The pain is going where the passion went.
> Few things will move you now to lose your head

And you can cause, or be caused, little harm.
Tonight you leave your audience content:
You were the ghost they wanted at the feast,
Though none of them recalls a word you said.

There's no 'Skype in full colour' here. It's a melancholy reflection. Even though 'things are simple now', since certitude has succeeded bewilderment, the poet finds himself in the dead calm. Nothing really can happen. You're not going to get angry about anything, you're not going to upset anyone. You've left your circle of friends feeling good about you. They wanted you to join them like Banquo's apparition but now you've gone they can't remember anything you said. There's also an implication that you had nothing to say anyway.

Many of us old old agers would find this pretty depressing. Certainly bewilderment is replaced by a new calm but that doesn't mean that nothing will happen; that passion is taken over by pain. All the old old agers, men and women alike, have an often untapped store of what was romantically called wisdom. This doesn't mean a capacity for being irrefutably right in matters of judgement or opinion. It means being able to bring accumulated experience to discerning appropriate direction.

Growing older doesn't mean only a diminution in one's ability to think through the business of human affairs. A precondition for the expression of wise responses is to be at ease with the concept of wonder. The elderly, if they are willing to so use it, have the leisure to devote time to contemplation, to 'thinking stuff', as grandchildren might put it, or the young and middle-aged call mindfulness. I may no longer be able to run to the car in a shower of rain but I can still have ideas in my head.

There's one thing that's been nagging at me in recent years. I wince when I hear of people (often celebs) say in interview; 'I'm not religious but I'm a spiritual person'. That expressed dichotomy is nonsense, it seems to me. There is such a response in human experience as the 'beyond self', a sense of mystery. There is the sensate, physical world, heat, cold, trees, clouds and there is that other world of 'why', where our sensations are inexplicable, outside or beyond the sharply logical. If we've been fortunate enough to observe a lunar eclipse, there are two kinds of reaction that we may have to the experience. One is logical: across the disc of the full moon is passing the shadow of the Earth. The other is (we may say) transcendental: there is something conjectural going on here; as the face of the moon darkens, we have a shiver of unknowing. As we age, and allow ourselves more time for contemplation, we are open to more experiences of the transcendent, that feeling of being outside our selves. I think that's religious and more than merely spiritual. The practice of 'thinking stuff' is an encouragement to wonder. Perhaps this is why at the bottom of all world religions is a yearning for transcendence.

Here are four ideas that I carry in my head, four ideas or notions that never fail to touch off a sense of wonder in me.

The exterior walls of our house are roughcast. At certain times of the year we find attached to the uneven texture of the walls the empty husks of cicadas. They are triggers to reflection. Cicadas lay their eggs in plant stems and the newly-hatched insects fall to the ground. Then they burrow with powerful forelegs into the soil, feeding on the roots of plants. Their development is very, very slow: in some species it may be seventeen years before the adults emerge. The male cicada has a small organ, rather like a set of drums, at the base of its abdomen and this can be made to vibrate 4,500 cycles per second. The result is a high-pitched screech, almost deafening: the Sydney poet, Christopher Brennan, got it just right when in a sonnet called 'Fire in the Heavens' he described the 'dazzling puncture … / In the cicada's torture point of song'. What I find marvellous about this life-cycle is that after years buried in the blank darkness, the pitch-black of the soil, the cicada emerges to scream ear-splittingly into the raw glare of the summer. Then, having joined with the female, it dies. There is no rationality here, no reason. And that's the wonder of it.

I can't imagine why the second idea took so long for me to become aware of. Quite recently I was reflecting on how the popularity in London of Montaigne's essays coincided with Shakespeare's later plays: both the essayist and the playwright had hit upon how fascinating were the individual's feelings and the expression of them. Nothing very remarkable here. But then there was another contemporary to enshrine human feelings and passions in graphic ways; it was the composer, Monteverdi. Monteverdi was a revolutionary in the same way that Montaigne and Shakespeare were. They worked and lived a mere two decades in common and in three different countries, Italy, France and England. Their coming together in the European consciousness was fortuitous if not downright random. All three of them were the first explorers in any thoroughgoing way of the world of feelings. I carry this with me as a significant idea because it alerts me to the possibility that similar comings-together may have similar important outcomes in science, medicine, IT and all the rest.

In my lifetime I've only ever met two seriously important people, celebrities. One was George Steiner, the literary and cultural critic. How we came to meet is not important here. Dorothy and I were having lunch in Geneva with Steiner (he was teaching there at the time), and at a casual and personal point in the conversation he asked us (it was Christmas week) where we were going to spend New Year. We thought we'd go by train via Florence to Siena, we said. 'Ah!' said Steiner, leaning forward, 'God is in Siena but He is not in Florence.' To me, to us, it was a striking observation, all the more because of its brevity. What Steiner had done in a mere ten words was to encapsulate an essential difference between the Middle Ages and the Renaissance. Walking the streets of Florence is a very different experience from walking the streets of Siena. The cities' cathedrals breathe theological and philosophical difference.

I've run on a bit with this history thing. Truth to tell,

I've never studied history either at school or university and I've always lamented that. I get a lot out of the landscape of history: my father had studied history and perhaps I caught something from him.

But to idea Number 4: the first stage in language development in young children is naming. They learn that objects in their world have a name and they can use that name when they point out the object. The child's toy bear is 'Teddy' and when the child sees Teddy and names him, a remarkable thing happens. Someone picks Teddy up and presents him to the child. The child therefore learns that if he wants something he can see, say, out of reach, the name does the trick. Naming what he can see on the other side of the room ensures that someone will put it within his grasp. So the child names the ball under the table and a duck in the bath. Soon another remarkable thing happens. Having learned to name a number of objects presented to him, then the child takes a most meaningful step and names something that isn't there. Teddy is in the child's bedroom and the child in the living room names the toy bear without it's being present. This is a huge leap in language-use. Teddy is conceptualised as an idea, not a present thing. The word itself conjures up an image of Teddy. Teddy was here: now Teddy is there (somewhere else). 'We left Teddy in the car'. The route from merely naming a visible Teddy to such an *idea* of Teddy somewhere else still astounds me. It keeps wonderment alive.

But what I've just done is recall past experiences, the

cicadas around the house, two historical transactions, and a reflection on language-development. It seems as though I've slipped into autobiography, something I never intended to do. We live in the opening decades of the new century and there's not been a time when so many people have been writing about themselves. As well as online expressions of self-hood like Facebook posts, blogs and tweets, there are diaries (I've quoted from one already), essays and full-blown memoirs. Whether this is a desperate lunge for notoriety in an unknown and fear-driven world or an obsession with self, I can't be sure. I note there is such a phenomenon as the serial memoirist: numbers of celebrity authors write as many as three and four or more autobiographies.

If in this brief account of old old age I sometimes slip or slide into memoir, I have to tell myself that I'm doing it because I want to be of some help to readers. What I'm trying to say here is that I understand because I've been there already and it's not as bad as you think. I'm wanting to point out that there are options and alternatives, that the mind is a fabulous resource in the way in which it processes and reprocesses experiences and ideas. I'm not thinking about crosswords, Sudoku or newspaper puzzles to keep the mind alert (useful though they may be). I'm after a willingness to enjoy notions which can be conjured up or which come into being unbidden. I've often visited friends who are seeing out their days in nursing homes. I'm familiar with the gathering-places in these facilities. As the residents wait for whatever entertainment is planned for the afternoon, they congregate, the able-bodied taking the seats nearest to the piano or the dais and the wheelchair-bound sit in semicircles behind them. Nothing is happening. The residents sit in silence. They stare ahead. No one knows what they're thinking, nor does anyone ever ask. They have been managed to this point in the day; they have not lived. This is a kind of benign cruelty operating here.

It's not for me here to run a commentary on aged care facilities. I can't really tell what they're like because I've never been in such places as a resident. My concern is for the other elderly who continue to live in their own homes or apartments and who are still more or less in command of their senses and their intellect.

One of the things I and numbers of my age-peers agree on is the lack of dignity afforded us. I don't mean teenagers standing up for us in a crowded tram or train. I mean twenty-somethings from the local government aged care helpline addressing us by our first names. When we were twenty-somethings ourselves, it would never have occurred to us to call Mrs Roberts Marjorie (even if we knew that was her name); we gave her the dignity of her social status. 'Good morning, Mrs Roberts' was the appropriate greeting. Our youth-obsessed society cares not a fig for dignity. We are all one. It's worse in a brief hospital stay, where nursing staff call us 'dear'. They treat us as though we are children. 'How are we this morning?' 'Hi Frank, things okay?' I think we have to fight against this; we've got to give better than we get.

There's a tendency with octogenarians to live within their own interiority. They wonder if anyone cares about what they think or if anyone is bothered to listen to them. They retreat into what they see as the safety of their own thinking and that's a great pity. Old old agers can't afford to lock themselves up in a cycle of their own reflections. They need to share their views of how they see the unfolding of the world about them. They will perhaps share their opinions with their age-peers (within whatever little community they are part of) but that's because they are assured of a listening ear. Otherwise they keep things to themselves. That's another pity. They need to talk to anybody and if anybody listens, that's really good.

There's a qualification here. As we age, we do tend to hold on to things we agree with, to lock ourselves into the known and the approved of. The proviso is that we keep alive an awareness of contrary opinion. It's comfortable for us to hear and read of principles that are our own but we also need in a deliberate way to attend to the expression of ideas we don't agree with. For example, there are certain newspaper columnists who espouse views contrary to mine. It's no answer to never read such journalists. Healthy ageing suggests we should expose ourselves to them from time to time to assure ourselves that we're not missing something. The same is true of radio and TV programmes. Otherwise how can we come to know how people can have views opposed to ours?

It all has to do with the alert mind. After a conversation with a member of our community group, I find it refreshing to be able to say to my wife, 'Well, what a sharp mind she has – she doesn't miss a trick' and there are more, many more like her. More than one would believe, given the press that the elderly get.

I belong to a social category that has escaped the crushing effects of mental impairment. I count myself extremely fortunate. I may sometimes find myself crabbed and cranky because my fingers can't twist a stiff door-handle, but I can still take extreme pleasure in a CD orchestral performance or a new novel. I just wish the media would recognise us.

It's interesting and encouraging for us to recognise that as our bodies decline, our minds for many (or most?) of us have a kind of coherence. The mind in an ageing body has continuity. We have learned a great deal over the years. If we have flexibility in the processing of our experiences, our attitudes and opinions undergo change. However, we ourselves remain essentially the person we always were. Despite passing through varieties of *personae*, we never lose touch with our real selves. But are we really in our 80s that real self and also someone else?

People want us to be different because we are old, whereas we want to be the same, but we're not. People who have only met us in our old age accept us as we appear to be, but we wish they'd known us in our prime. So it goes. We used to see life stretching ahead of us. We never thought, barring accidents, that it would ever end. Now, however, the end is in sight. Time, in terms of our existence, no longer lies ahead of us but lies behind. We're left with memories and have lost our sense of anticipation. Or so we are told.

I'm not sure that we need to strike expectancy from our lexicon. It's possible, surely, for old old agers to look forward to things, going to a movie or having lunch with friends. It depends on the quality of our hopefulness.

In *Love in the Time of Cholera*, Gabriel Garcia Marquez sees the notion of ageing as like this:

> Age has no reality except in the physical world. The essence of a human being is resistant to the passage of time. Our inner lives are eternal, which is to say that our spirits remain as youthful and vigourous as when we were in full bloom.

– 9 –

In My End Is My Beginning

It doesn't take much to make the elderly happy. To receive a handful of greeting cards on a birthday is a pleasure. Little gestures, like phone calls or texts, lighten ageing spirits. Remember Lady Slane who didn't want visits from children or grandchildren? Towards the end of the novel she establishes a rare relationship with her radical and independent great-granddaughter, Deborah; the mutual understanding they have for each other is touching and magically profound across three generations. I can relate to a linkage like that; I have held a great-grandson in my arms. I cannot begin to find words to describe the emotions that flickered through me as I nodded in response to his smile, watched his twinkling eyes open wide, then close into deep, deep sleep. Holding him, I was very happy. The inner life of the elderly, however, is a seesaw. I suppose I imagined when I was young-old that I would eventually enter upon some wise calm, docking in the harbour that Epicurus foresaw.

But there are times when I feel absolutely rotten. For no good reason, I must say, I wake up and I just know it's going to be one of those days. I can't open the fresh carton of milk for our morning coffee and milk squirts all over the kitchen bench and I just know. By the time the afternoon has come around, I can't cope any more. I've fallen out with my wife over some footling and unimportant matter and I feel my life is flying to pieces. My world is shifting on its axis. I'm anxious because I sense that I'm not in control. Our generation didn't know about the kind of anxiety we now find ourselves living in. We are caught up in an epidemic of anxiousness. We get into the habit of asking ourselves those 'what if?' questions. What if my part-pension is reduced? What if my breathlessness is the precursor to a serious health issue? What if I'm eating the wrong things? What if my arthritis worsens? How can I deal with these fairly pointless questions?

As we get older we have to fall back on whatever courage we can muster. We need that courage to face the reality of mortality. We've got to confront the truth of what is to be hoped for and the truth of what is to be feared. That's difficult. It's not something easily dealt with at the end of life. But it's followed by another kind of courage, which is the courage to act upon the truth we find. We have to decide whether our hopes or our fears are what should matter most, to ourselves and to those we love. Choice is one of the nuts for the old old folks to crack. Making decisions is hard for us. It starts in the supermarket: there are a dozen breakfast cereals to choose from, or six kinds of mustard, or five kinds of paper towels. It shouldn't matter all that much, but for the elderly it seems it does. Faced with a choice, we are inclined to say, even desperately, 'Oh, I don't know' and hope someone will decide for us. My wife wants to know whether she should wear her blue top or the red one. We've lost much of our capacity for making up our minds. This is why, for some of us, other people like our children think it's their right to make decisions on our behalf, like where we should live in retirement, or where we should go for a holiday. Or even more sensitive issues.

In her novel, *They May Not Mean To, But They Do*, Cathleen Schine offers a vivid portrait of Joy Bergman and her children, Molly and Daniel. Joy has nursed her much-loved husband through lengthy incontinence and dementia and later the family rally around her in her widowhood. What they don't appreciate is Joy's loneliness. By chance on her regular walk in the neighbourhood park she meets Karl with his carer. Karl is an old school-friend, now widower, and the two of them develop a friendship, to the irritation of Molly and Daniel. Joy is staying with the children in the family holiday-house and her relationship with Karl is under heated discussion.

> 'You think he can take dad's place?' Molly said, all pretence at civility gone. 'Well he can't. Ever.'
>
> She was shouting now, and Daniel stomped down the stairs to join in: 'The body is not even cold. How can you do this to us?'

Joy looked away from them, her two beloved children, yelling and stamping their feet like toddlers. Greying toddlers. She tilted her head back and looked at the ceiling and wondered if it might fall in and shut them up.

'What has Karl ever done to you?' she said softly.

There was silence, just the thunder, closer now and the rain on the roof.

'Do you know that Karl asked me to live with him?'

'See?' Daniel said to Molly. 'See? I told you.'

'Mommy! You can't. You'll turn into a caretaker.'

'Your father liked Karl. Your father would have wanted me to have some companionship. Your father would be ashamed of you both.'

They shifted uneasily.

'Yeah, well, still, it's just…' Daniel's words trailed off.

'And whether I choose to live with Karl or not,' Joy continued, 'one thing I can see clearly now. I cannot stay in this house one day longer. I am not welcome. I do not belong.'

And she marched out, slammed her door, and began packing.

This is the kind of situation that is not common, but not uncommon, either. Joy's children are not coping with their father's death and the grief blinds them to their mother's desolation. They are feeling for themselves. 'How can you do this to us?' They are simply another generation.

They want to make Joy's choices for her, but she needs to make them for herself.

When I was a schoolteacher, I soon found in my colleagues exemplars of the aphorism, 'a man among boys and a boy among men'. It's always been a puzzle to me how experience seems to bypass some people. I have a number of acquaintances, young-olds and older who behave like teenagers, make silly and unfunny remarks, seem to have no sense of dignity in social situations, as if life has barely touched them, or they've learned nothing from it. They give us old old agers a bad name. I'd like to think that to survive into the 80s would confer some wisdom and some right of choice. When bad stuff happens to us we learn something about the world that we didn't know before and we should store that something away for future reference. Whatever the trauma is, physical, emotional, psychological, it's part of learning to be. In a general sense, whatever the circumstances are, octogenarians have by the fact of their very survival earned being treated with dignity, not being written off as 'past it'. I don't think I'm 'past it'. I have many acquaintances of my age who are certainly 'with it'. We can still contribute acceptable opinion in contemporary debate.

When I began thinking about this little book, I determined I wouldn't fall back or even lean on surveys or study results. As my writing time went by, I came to realise that to ignore old age research was no great matter because it tended to be restricted to young-olds and olds and very rarely to old olds. Only one study I've come across has dealt specifically with the 85+ cohort. This study explored the common assumptions about the lives of octogenarians: people of old old age often have at least one family member to support them; the well-being of people of this age requires social activity; successful adaptation to age-related life changes demands a continuity of self-concept. The researchers found the sample suggested all three assumptions were false. This age-cohort didn't have family-members to support them, having often out-lived them (a quarter of the sample had no family-member support). The sample were not activity-oriented but welcomed increased detachment from social contact. And there were 'changes in their cognitive and emotional processes that reconstituted their self-representation', to use the language of the report.

As a member of this age-group and having talked to age-peers about being part of it, I can give assent to their findings. Yes, sure, we don't all have family-members we can rely on for practical and emotional support. We don't always want to be part of friendship-gatherings but often prefer to be left to our own thoughts or pastimes; happiness in old age is not proportional to physical activity in the company of others. And as we age, even modes of thinking and feeling undergo changes and the self we present to others is modified. 'You've changed as you've got older', people say, and of course they're right.

Old age, especially old old age, needn't be a stagnant pool which our lives have flowed into. There is a current shifting beneath the surface, refreshing the water.

Ageing is often seen in negative terms. It's the process whereby everything closes down. Physical frailty saps us of emotional strength and the renewal of ourselves becomes improbable, unlikely. Or so it is commonly believed by the elderly.

In Dominic Smith's *The Last Painting of Sara de Vos* there is a character waiting to survive his 80s who's a wealthy New York lawyer.

> He carries the past around like a bottle of antacids in his pocket. You outlive your wife, then your colleagues and friends, then your accountant and building doorman. You no longer attend the opera, because the human bladder can only endure so much. Social engagements require strategy and hearing-aid calibrations. Every sports coat you own is too big because you continue to shrink, your shoulders like a rumour behind all that fabric. You are waiting to die without ever thinking about death itself. It's a face at the window, peering in.

This is Monty DeGroot. He's old old, all right. He senses death watching him. In his hotel room he leaves the lights on all night. There is no possibility of renewal here. And, yes, there are lots of us who believe it'll be like this. But it doesn't have to be so. It's a matter of one's mind-set. There are olds and old olds who lament the things they can no longer do and retreat from the everyday. Admittedly it requires an effort of the will but it's far more healthy for the 80+ group, women and men, to represent themselves than for them to languish in memories that already have a sepia tinge to them. We can re-present ourselves by always being open to what is new to us, reading biographies and watching documentaries, being curious about the world. New experiences have the capacity to enliven us, refresh us. There's certainly no reason why as we age we have to let go.

Recently I tried something new. A friend of mine (admittedly younger than I) encouraged me to seek mindfulness as a means of clearing my head of muddle and suggested a simple exercise. Sit in a firm chair in the kitchen or the dining room, feet flat on the floor, back straight, eyes closed, open hands on one's lap and breathe deeply, in in six breaths, hold, and out in three, having cleared the mind of everything except the breathing pattern and focusing on that alone, 1 2 3 4 5 6, 1 2 3, 1 2 3 4 5 6, 1 2 3. I find this exercise a sure way of emptying my buzzing head in a timed seven minutes or so. Afterwards when I stand and walk about the room I am enlivened, I am refreshed, I am open. It works for me.

As we age, it ought to be easier for us to be honest and straightforward. We ought to be past feeling we have to tiptoe around ideas and opinions. There comes a point when we have to face where we are at and be prepared to say it like it is. We could compile a list of things we need to watch out for: not to be obsessed with health issues, or to get grumpy over little things going wrong; not to feel sorry for oneself or feel guilty over things not done. In the contracted world of the octogenarian it's difficult not to be near-consumed by minor issues. Unless we're careful, the humdrum and monotonous take on an importance they don't deserve; minor becomes major. It's because there's not enough in our heads, and the vacant spaces fill up with negatives. It's not the answer to try to be cheerful all the time. That way madness lies. We need balance.

I can well understand how elderly people who live with intense pain find their thoughts turning often to some time when the pain is no more; they reach peaks of suffering that have them willing it to all end. For me, and for people like me, who've been spared such ongoing pain, the questions surrounding the end of life seldom occur. While we can still survive month by month with a clear head and a body which functions with minimum discomfort, we don't dwell on our own death. We visit friends in hospitals in acute care units, we attend more funerals than we wish we were obliged to, but we just don't think of death visiting us. Perhaps in our 80s we should.

Apparently the old old are not very likely to die suddenly, as with a massive stroke, nor to die from a terminal illness, having survived as long as they have. Actually they're not likely to die from organ failure, either. More than half of us will die from sheer frailty. When you live to what is sometimes called 'a great age', it's not surprising that your physical totality will ease into some neutral way of being and finally run down altogether. What this means to many of us is that we've got time to contemplate the inevitability of it all. Time even to talk about it with someone, spouse, partner, family, friends, and in that talking make plans; what's going to happen to your father's fob watch and chain, or your mother's wedding ring? You can start with things like that not specified in a will and then lead on to larger issues. Your children and grandchildren won't, don't want to discuss anything to do with your death. It's stressful enough for them to see your increasing decrepitude, but talk we must, to avoid the later 'if only…' and 'I wish I …' regrets.

I suppose when we used the phrase, 'a good death', we mean an unfussy death, dying in one's bed at home, or not waking up from a doze in an armchair or subsiding peacefully onto the back lawn while picking some flowers but what then? Have we just, as it were, entered a final sleep? Are we (in a dream?), as Hamlet puts it, in 'The undiscover'd country from whose bourne/no traveller returns'? Or in a heaven where we shall meet relatives and friends who died before us and are waiting to receive us into an eternal reunion or a galactic immensity of black blankness or… we cannot know. Scores of metaphors and similes from scores of religious world-views offer no certainty. What do I think is going to happen to me when I die?

Death can't afford to be proud (John Donne's phrase) because death isn't the end. My father lives in me, I live in my sons, I live in my daughter. I live in my grandsons, my granddaughters, my great-grandson. I believe people live on in the lives they've touched and in the memories that people have of them in a greater consciousness. I believe (don't ask me how or why) there is an all-encompassing 'mind of God' and in that infinite mind of God we all live on totally and forever. The infallible memory of this God holds us. This is our immortality, the books of our lives filed away. That's my grand metaphor, my personal meaning of death. I can't expect anyone to believe what I believe, but to have something to believe gives meaning to existence. I've come to terms with myself. From chubby childhood (as photographs tell me) through to adult retirement I can recall and relive a life crammed with mistakes, joys, sorrows and things brought to being and I come face-to-face with one of ageing's great contradictions: for us to reach back into the past we have to go through the future. What octogenarians do is to lean on that future. Chubby childhood beginnings and walking-stick endings are equally mysterious.

In the previous chapter I recalled having in my lifetime met only two great literary minds: one was George Steiner. The other was the American novelist, John Updike. As with Steiner, how Updike and I came to meet is not important here. A metre or so of my bookshelves filled with Updike novels, short stories and essays attests to the years of my reading him. He was a powerful chronicler of modern America and his narratives were set firmly in contemporary US history.

Updike's finest work is the life of Harry (Rabbit) Angstrom: it runs into a tetralogy, four rich volumes of contemporary existence, the last of which is called *Rabbit at Rest*. Rabbit reached the pinnacle of his life's achievement as a brilliant college basketballer and thereafter we trace him as a car salesman in middle America, a bigot and chauvinist, vulgar and mundane and an adulterer, a failure as a father and hoping to be better as a grandfather. And this is how he dies, after foolishly playing basketball with some Negro street youths, in an acute care hospital room after a massive heart attack, with family around him, his son Nelson rabidly anxious:

> 'We phoned Aunt Mim, Dad, and she'll get here as soon as she can. She has to change planes in Kansas City!' From his expression and the pitch of his voice, the boy is shouting into a fierce wind blowing from his father's direction. 'Don't *die*, Dad, *don't!*' he cries, then sits back with that question still on his face, and his dark wet eyes shining like stars of a sort. Harry shouldn't leave the question hanging like that, the boy depends on him. 'Well, Nelson,' he says, 'all I can tell you is, it isn't so bad!' Rabbit thinks he should maybe say more, the kid looks wildly expectant, but enough. Maybe. Enough.

The question on Nelson's face is why does his dad have to die, despite all his parental shortcomings. The desperation in the son's outburst reminds me of Les Murray's poem on his father's death, 'The Last Hellos' and the anguished cries in it: 'Don't die, Dad – / but they do' and 'Don't die, Cecil / But they do.' Rabbit Angstrom's last words are the best reassurance he can offer to his son, 'It isn't too bad'. One of the gifts of old age is to be able to alert the next generation to the fact that it is an ending, a finality and for life to be worthwhile there needs to be the awareness that there is an end. We owe it to those who come after.

That's why the begging 'Don't die' is, I think, ultimately not very helpful. Death isn't a loss; a transition, maybe, but not a loss. As it may be put, death is like birth. It changes the world and changes reality in the most profound of ways. One moment there is a living, breathing someone there and the next moment the way we relate to that someone is irrevocably and irretrievably changed. But somewhere there is an echo of that someone, something for us to hang onto.

– 10 –

Epilogue

Old old age ends in all sorts of ways. Is it possible to imagine how much we have accumulated over a near-lifetime? A dinner set with several bread-and-butter plates missing and only four of six champagne glasses; a school prize; a tennis racket hanging at the back of a garage; years of tax returns; a blunt can-opener; a torn beach umbrella, also in the garage. And who is to get rid of it all? We should have thrown it out ages ago. It's all a grand metaphor. At the end of life this accumulation of experience does clutter up our thinking. There are many things we seem unable to let go, attitudes especially, feelings. We need to get a lot of our living out into a skip and have it carted away. We have enough to deal with as it is.

It's all new, old old age. What this guidebook has been wanting to do is to suggest it doesn't have to be dark and forbidding and wearisome. It's not the dying that's the issue for me but it's the process. Not the event itself, but the years, months or weeks that precede it, and how the process may affect family and friends. For my part, I'd be pleased as the light fades to see in my hands pearls of great price that have marked my life. As a mystic might have said, 'We need to live gently with the big questions'.

When Death gets to be a face at the window, peering in, we find ourselves wondering what all our living has meant. What has life been all about? The question comes to us whether we are alone in an apartment or in a nursing home or even if we're still with the company of a partner. It's sad that nobody has time to sit with us and listen while we try to wrestle some sense out of all that we have been. What have we discovered about living itself, about other people, about the way human relationships work? Does anybody want to hear from us?

Some of us, probably most of us of our generation have already watched the dying of the light in the eyes of those we've loved. For some of them, it was a gentle going into that good night; for others, there was pain that was sharp and scarcely eased by palliative care; or physical exhaustion from just taking one breath after another. We can only wonder how it will be for us. It's a struggle with the one fact of our lives about which none of us has doubts and yet we're never quite ready to face. We treasure more and more the simple pleasures, reflect more and more on our joys and feel grateful for what we have known of love.

It's strange how our lives in old old age come full circle. We drift into being children again. We get anxious when we're left alone, like children. We crave lovingness and care, like children. We want to be told we're doing well, like children. We need to feel safe, like children.

Over forty-five years ago I had a professional relationship with Bruce Dawe, probably the most genuinely popular poet in 20th century Australia. Relationships like ours inevitably shift into pleasant memories. In the intervening years I would come across a Dawe poem in a magazine or newspaper and remember. Now, as I brought this little book to a close, I came across another one. You have to understand that Bruce is only a year younger than I am: in a real sense you can hear the voices of others of our age in his poem, 'Walking Our Dog'.

> *To know no more of nights and days*
> *puzzles me still,*
> *like the child who (perforce) in the cupboard lays*
> *those toys and contrivances that still*
> *are dear to him, however much*
> *they've also meant to others who before*
> *his time (O long before!) had loved to touch,*
> *to hold and treasure.*
> *Walking our dog (the latest*
> *of that family I've known) for many a measure*
> *I think of those others who*
> *survived it all, and in turn left*
> *it all behind, just as we, too,*
> *must leave, some sooner and some late,*
> *as though the mother of all life should come*
> *and 'Tchk, tchk' say, 'Why, look, it's after eight,*

and past your bedtime … Come,
put all those playthings by … That's right!',
then tuck you in for that last sleep
and that longest most mysterious night …

Our cupboards are full of recalled experiences that were dear to us and that sustain us, and sooner or later we'll have to leave them behind. It's past our bedtime.

We can't rely on psychologists, philosophers, sociologists, or theologians to guide us at the very end. Only the painters, musicians, novelists and poets can give us calm entry into that mysterious night.

About the Author

Four generations of Hansens

Dr Ian Hansen taught in schools in Australia and for five years in England and was invited to join the then Faculty of Education at Melbourne University where he taught for almost thirty years, retiring as Associate Professor. He published numerous books and articles on the teaching of English, a book of poems, a memoir and with his wife, Dorothy, four institutional histories and two biographies. He has three children, seven grandchildren and one great-grandson. He has an abiding interest in theology, Persian rugs, the Victorians and poetry.

CPSIA information can be obtained
at www.ICGtesting.com
Printed in the USA
BVHW030649030720
582586BV00003B/261